CONCILIUM

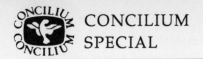

CONCILIUM
SPECIAL

FUNDAMENTALISM AS AN ECUMENICAL CHALLENGE

Edited by

Hans Küng and
Jürgen Moltmann

SCM Press · London

0 334 02648 2

First published 1992 by SCM Press
9-17 St Albans Place London N1 0NX
as the 1992/3 issue of the journal Concilium
This reissue 1996

Typeset at The Spartan Press Ltd, Lymington, Hants
Printed and bound in Great Britain by
Biddles Ltd, Guildford and King's Lynn

Contents

Preface

Fundamentalism as an Ecumenical Challenge

The word fundamentalism was originally used for a particular trend in American Protestantism which in the face of all modern and liberal adaptations of the church sought to go back to the biblical 'fundamentals' of the Christian faith: to fundamentals of faith which were interpreted in a very arbitrary way. Developments in Christianity in our time have shown that fundamentalist symptoms and developments analogous to this movement within Protestantism can also be found in the sphere of Roman Catholicism and Eastern Orthodoxy. Indeed, in our day the term 'fundamentalism' has also been transferred to reactionary trends within Islam and Judaism. That is reason enough for taking the ecumenical dimension of this problem seriously and reflecting on it in depth.

This issue is concerned to give as precise and lively a picture as possible of this development, in a great variety of spheres of the church and religion. It does not disqualify the fundamentalist trends from the start, but does all it can to try to understand the causes of the rise of fundamentalism. For fundamentalism is a challenge to all religions and confessions which can no longer be overlooked, and which must be taken with intellectual seriousness. Individuals, groups and peoples will not be able to live in peace if those who have commandeered the 'fundamentals' for themselves believe that they can deny others the right to exist, or if non-fundamentalists do all they can to exclude fundamentalists or in intellectual arrogance simply pass them by. There will be no peace without a readiness for understanding on both sides.

So this issue is concerned to provide objective information, critical illumination and strategies for dealing with the problem of fundamentalism. We begin by defining the term in a way which brings together perspectives from theology, social psychology, psychiatry and sociology. We then go on to analyse Jewish and Islamic fundamentalism. For

Christian fundamentalism we hear voices from Orthodoxy, Roman Catholicism and Protestantism. Then in two syntheses we ourselves, as editors of this volume, state our positions: the one more in terms of theological principle from a Protestant perspective ('Fundamentalism and Modernity'), the other more in terms of practical church politics from a Catholic perspective in the style of a plea 'Against Contemporary Roman Catholic Fundamentalism'.

Jürgen Moltmann
Hans Küng

I · Definition

What is Fundamentalism?
Theological Perspectives

Martin E. Marty

1. The emergence of fundamentalist oppositionalism

The fundamental theological feature of modern fundamentalisms which are religious – there are other kinds as well – is oppositionalism. Fundamentalism in any context takes form when members of already conservative or traditional movements experience threat. Something or someone, be it modernity or modernism, secularization or the West, the infidel or the Great Satan, attacks their culture, their group, their very selves. The foe from without or the compromiser or traitor from within is perceived as fighting them. They fight back.[1]

Fighting back as a constitutive principle determines the shape of fundamentalist theological methods, principles and substance, just as it does the shape of fundamentalist group formation and political strategy. Fundamentalists may share with conservatives, moderates or liberals a positive love of scriptures and tradition; what they possess distinctively is a peculiar pattern of oppositionalism. Their agenda is set by what they feel or calculate demands their resistance, by what they must contend against, by their aversions and antagonisms. This aspect of their programme colours everything they do, including those things which are or appear to be positive elements of witness or behaviour.

To isolate oppositionalism is not to insult or distort any fundamentalism. The founders of the most familiar sorts of each, which take rise in 'religions of the book', where there is an easily accessible canon which can serve as an authority, announced their original programmes as theological calls to arms. Whether the Torah, the Qur'an (or the corollary laws of the Sharia'), or the Hebrew scriptures plus the New Testament provides the charter and reference point, the code of tenets and practices drawn from such texts is arranged to be most effective to advance oppositionalism.

What follows is an elaboration of this thesis, based on tentative conclusions drawn from the most ambitious effort yet made to study and compare fundamentalisms around the world, one sponsored by the American Academy of Arts and Sciences. Comparative studies have as their built-in hazard a temptation to cluster and lump together highly diverse phenomena. But their compensatory asset, which issues from the rationale for comparativism in the first place, is to help the scholar see elements which might be elusive were only one instance of a phenomenon to be studied. Those two sentences impel the writing of this one: fundamentalisms in different religions necessarily and inevitably have nothing in common in respect to theological substance. Each exists, among other things, for their leaders and members to create distance from and antagonism to the claims of other faiths. There may be a common theological reference point in Allah, Yahweh, and the God of Jesus Christ, but fundamentalists would be the least likely factions in the various faith communities to acknowledge the validity of such a proposition or to experience common witness or worship.

To make oppositionalism the key mark of theology is to risk violating what anthropologists seek when they speak of 'agents' description'. By that they mean that a good phenomenologist listens closely and provides accurate accounting based on the perceptions and declarations of an actor in the group being studied. It is not likely that an interviewer of, say, a member of a Protestant fundamentalist movement, who asked her why she was in it, would hear: 'Because we perceived a threat to our core identity as traditionalist Christians and found it necessary to react.' More likely she would say: 'Because I am "born again"; I found Jesus, repented of my sins, love God, and want to convert a fallen world, including you!' At the same time, however, so consistent is the witness of members and leaders to their antagonist stance, born of the occasion which gave rise to their movement, that it does no injustice to concentrate on it; indeed, it illumines all aspects of theology.

In what follows there will be no reference to the fundamentalisms that have taken rise among radical and extremist Hindus, Buddhists, Neoconfucians, or other Asian religionists, though these have all seen 'fundamentalist-like movements'. The accent here is on the Abrahamic, Jerusalemaic, 'peoples of the Book'. Constraints of space and my own familiarity with Christianity dictate that the main illustrations will come from the prevalent Protestant fundamentalism which issued largely from the United States and Canada in the 1920s and to a lesser extent on subsequent Catholic fundamentalisms. Islam and Judaism will appear chiefly for comparison, but they will be elaborated elsewhere in this volume.[2]

2. The Rejection of Hermeneutics

Fundamentalism as a theological oppositionalism necessarily initiates its programme with propaedeutic and prolegomenal issues. These do not represent formalities, a mere waiting in the anteroom next to the hall where serious theological discourse will proceed. Instead, these issues are as central for fundamentalism as for all other theological movements.

At the very beginning, then, come hermeneutical issues; modern theology is hermeneutically-informed from first to last. Fundamentalism is therefore anti-hermeneutical. The Haredi or ultra-Orthodox in Jerusalem and the Gush Emunim, the militants in the Bloc of the Faithful, are as sure of their literal following of divine revelation and rabbinic law as Shi'ite Muslim fundamentalists in Iran have been when they literally applied *shari'a* to transgressors of Islamic codes. The Catholic members of Communione e Liberazione in Italy, the Lefebvrists in France and elsewhere, and the North American and Latin American Catholic fundamentalists who express love-hate relations with Protestant fundamentalists, never heard of Scottish common sense realism and probably are, or think they are, heirs of some version of Thomist traditions. But they share with the Protestants the claim that a text, however difficult and mysterious, because it is a revelation of God, is accessible and admits of but one meaning.

In fundamentalist understandings, fallible humans, including fundamentalists, may not always know how to overcome apparent contradictions in a text. They will admit that they may not yet have resolved all difficulties among themselves. But the notion that symbols are multivocal; that the presuppositions which readers bring to texts colour their interpretations of those texts; the sense that the interpretation of the whole colours the rendering of each part of a text and that each 'passage' of scripture has to be seen in the light of the interpretation of the larger whole – foundational elements in modern hermeneutics – are lost on fundamentalists or are occasions for resistance and oppositionalism.

In the framework of Paul Ricoeur's famous treatment of criticism or interpretation, there are several choices. One may lose faith when criticism comes. Or a believer – and this could be called the liberal option or necessity – may 'believe only by interpreting, using a "second naivete".'[3] But fundamentalists instinctively live, or they choose to live, with a form of faith that exists '*in spite of interpretation*'. Everyone around them insists on perspectivalism in reading of texts; everyone else recognizes that for all the efforts at phenomenological bracketing which sophisticates undertake, the assumptions born of experience and locked in human subjectivity never wholly disappear. They help predetermine readings of the texts by which the community lives.

Fundamentalist theology in the classic Protestant school was born in the shadow of Princeton Seminary. Many scholars, most notably Ernest Sandeen and George Marsden, have traced the influence of a particular approach which was so decisive in producing fundamentalism that most fundamentalists do not even recognize it. In José Ortega y Gasset's terms, Baconian inductivism and Scottish common sense realism represent fundamentalist *creencias*, ideas which are so close that one does not know one holds them; they are not the ideas one 'has' but the ideas that one 'is'.[4]

Briefly, since Baconian inductivism combined with Scottish common sense realism is not coin of the philosophical realm far outside Protestant fundamentalist intellectual circles, it should be explained that this approach argues that ordinary people making ordinary use of their senses can gain knowledge of the real world, if they act responsibly. With it the nineteenth-century Protestants, in a tradition that lived on among antecedents of fundamentalism, became extremely self-confident about their hold on truth. They needed only one assumption and, some would say, one miracle: if God is a God of love and truth, God will reveal God's self, necessarily in a form available to ordinary people with eyes and ears and senses. God, it is then declared, has done so in the canonical scriptures. The task of the theologian, then, is to co-ordinate the historical and literary 'facts' of the Bible and order them systematically. It can be seen that in this case, as in many other religions, fundamentalism is very rationalistic, though its rationalism counters the more regularly supported post-Enlightenment academic rationalisms.[5]

The fundamentalist who encounters admitted hermeneuts is either bemused or scornful: how can you read the text I do, and not come to the same understanding of it as I? You must be operating in the bad faith which characterizes liberalism and which compromises or alters the divine word.[6] The fundamentalist in reacting this way may be doing so in good faith, making a serious effort to introduce or, as he or she would put it, reintroduce absolutes and the authoritative Word on the theological scene. Follow such absolute and authoritative readings, says the fundamentalist, and we can agree. We will have made a contribution to clarifying the life of the believing community, to reducing the options embodied there. One needs only a lightly developed sense of irony to see what happens in these cases: the rest of the theological community, the members of the believing community who shun the invitations of a fundamentalist camp that lives off it, treat such contentions hermeneutically; the fundamentalist, then, in the act of clarifying the community and reducing the options, has only muddied things by adding one more.

The antihermeneutical intuition and posture is the cause of frustration between those who would engage in theological conversation with fundamentalists and the fundamentalists themselves. Such conversation therefore normally goes on only in familial settings, or in confrontations between ecclesiastical factions and citizen groups; fundamentalists tend to take on non-fundamentalists in formal theology only through polemical journals and almost never through open encounter. This is especially the case if a discourse is to be truly dialogical, with the implication of risk that someone might change his mind. What, asks the fundamentalist, is to be undertaken in conversation, which is designed to effect change in all parties? In sum: expect an exchange of witnesses, not a mutual probing if and when a forum for theological interchange is established.

3. The rejection of pluralism and relativism

Accompanying the assault on hermeneutics is a second aspect of fundamentalist oppositionalism: the tendency to fuse and then reject pluralism and relativism as if the fundamentalist can stand above the 'many' and not be victim of the erosive character of perspectival or relativist thought. This is not to say that fundamentalist pioneers were never aware of pluralism. It is indeed such a standard feature of whatever passes for modernity that no one can evade seeing it. But the recognition of its presence as a threat was an occasion for the rise of fundamentalism.

Here fundamentalism again differed from traditionalism, which represented pluralistic ignorance, or conservatism, which was a kind of passive distancing from the 'other', who lived in another valley, heeded the call of a different set of church bells, and would be a threat only were there to be positive contact.

Modernity brings contact. The other lives next door. The other sends subversive signals through mass media whose signals one cannot easily escape. Modern polity provides the legal basis for pluralism by assuring that all voices have rights to express themselves. It is the recognition of this freedom by the Second Vatican Council that was among the specific eventuations which kept the Lefebvrists from accepting that Council. The college of bishops in the Declaration on Religious Freedom recognized the legal rights of those in error. Even worse, the hated pluralism was increasingly evident also within the church, whether this meant the Baptist or Presbyterian denominations of the 1920s or Catholicism after the mid-1960s and the end of the Council. The propounded notion that one can 'live and let live' with a variety of interpretations under one *magisterium*, within one dogmatic tradition, or inside one ecclesiastical jurisdiction, is exactly what led fundamentalists to fight back.

Pluralism, the allowance for and the potential of listening to various possibly legitimate contentions, had as its inevitable corollary, in fundamentalist eyes, an endorsement of relativism. Such a connection is not integral; many philosophers have shown how one may recognize legal and even ecclesiastical pluralism without falling into relativism. Sir Isaiah Berlin and the British philosopher Ernest Gellner have spent considerable energy opposing the idea that all pluralism leads to mere relativism. Father John Courtney Murray, S J, already in the years before the Council, demonstrated one way – not the only way, other Catholic theologians would say – for the faithful to recognize pluralism but to be firmly anti-relativist.[7]

Still, the fundamentalist instinct is not all wrong. Most modern theology takes into consideration, along with hermeneutics, the plurality of theological viewpoints and the recognition that these, asserted at once, can well issue in an endorsement of perspectival or relativist thought. At the very least, it has involved something along Alfred Schutz's lines which recognize 'multiple realities' and differing 'systems of relevance'.[8] The same person may hold within himself a variety of viewpoints, and will express them variously, depending upon what focus of attention is momentarily at issue. Such a recognition was abhorrent to the founders of fundamentalism. In the factionalized Northern Baptist and Presbyterian denominations in the United States of the 1920s, when the first round of fundamentalist controversy erupted, as well as in the more recent pre-schisms in the Lutheran Church – Missouri Synod and the Southern Baptist Convention, the fundamentalist party, naturally finding actual liberalisms (in the 1920s cases) or putative liberalisms (in the 1970s instances) abhorrent, put their energies into attacking the 'live and let live' moderates and compromisers. These majoritarians had wanted to encompass both the fundamentalist and the modernist or liberal factions. That would mean an endorsement of a pluralism within the church which represented to fundamentalists the end of theological seriousness. It also meant a relativism that would corrode the very reasons one would have for being a Christian and a member of a particular denominations. So they fought back and arranged oppositional theology.

4. Against evolution and development

After the impasses over hermeneutics, pluralism and relativism, the fundamentalist theological oppositionalism appeared in the development of philosophies of history. These are implicit in all systematic theologies and explicit in those which are intended to deal with controversies over beginnings and ends of history and of meaning in the meantime. Arthur Danto has made a distinction between analytic philosophy of history, which all historians, all thoughtful people, fashion all the time, and substantive philosophy of history, in which people use macro- or metahistorical outlooks to identify with some precision where history began and where it is going.[9]

As for beginnings, in such substantive philosophies of history, fundamentalism took rise in the century after Darwin, and as a firmly oppositional statement against evolution and development. Evolutionary theory in science, in the eyes of fundamentalists, gave abhorrent, anti-scriptural, and thus patently false accountings of universal origins, including the human condition. When adaptive theologians began to embrace evolution as an historical understanding and thus as more than a mere biological and natural hypothesis, fundamentalists reacted and fought back. In the United States some have invented a movement called 'Creation Research', designed to refute evolution, to counter it in the public-school classrooms, and to contend for it as an alternative to mainstream science in the laboratory. Creationists, as they call themselves, cannot regard the evolutionary outlook of other Christians as being legitimately reflexive; they see it as wilful denial of the evidences God left in nature and of the testimonies Genesis carries in the book.

Roman Catholic fundamentalists have made little of opposition to natural evolution; that battle is less a part of their history, especially since the core texts for Catholic fundamentalists are not scriptural. The dismissal of the cosmic theological evolutionism of thinkers like Pierre Teilhard de Chardin at mid-century occurred on the basis of reasoning that was by no means restricted to reference to Genesis – though some dispute over monogenism in Roman Catholicism did make reference to the literal interpretation of Genesis stories about a single original human pair.

More regularly, the Catholic extremist contention is not over biological evolution but over historical development in respect to ordinary secular history and, inside the church, *the magisterium* and its custodianship. Catholic fundamentalist root documents are more likely to have issued from the papacy between the Council of Trent and the eve of the Second Vatican Council. Recent popes, including the cautious Paul VI and the ultraconservative John Paul II, are seen as betrayers of the tradition which produced Tridentine definitions and canons, the Syllabus of Errors, and the statements on authority in the first Vatican Council. John Henry Newman and Johann Adam Möhler may have pioneered with theological or Hegelian concepts of doctrinal development, while some notion of development colours most Catholic historical inquiry and much theological formulation. Not, however, for the Catholic fundamentalist, who regards Catholic truth as a set of truths deposited once and for all. They may be expounded in different ways in different cultures, but there can be no development of doctrine.

5. In favour of apocalyptic millennialism

As with beginnings of history, so with ends: most fundamentalisms propose rather precise envisionings of the end and judgments about it. Substantive philosophy of history, says Arthur Danto, deals with the future as if it had already occurred – at least enough to provide colouring for interpreting the meantime.

Fundamentalisms are oppositional theologies which, at least in the West, resisted Enlightenment progressivisms, developmentalisms and socialisms like the Marxist project. For most American Protestants and, in their wake, Protestant fundamentalists everywhere, millennialism became attractive. They repudiated amillennial views, because with them one was not sure where history was going. They also rejected the postmillennialism which had dominated American Protestant theology for the century after the 1740s, when Jonathan Edwards and others began to propose it.

In place of these, fundamentalists have favoured oppositional and apocalyptic premillennialism.[10] With it one makes clear in the face of progressivisms that God is in control of history, and that the fundamentalist community authoritatively has a purchase on the future denied all others. With it one has an impulse to convert others, to rescue them from a world that does not recognize a *kairos* in the midst of ordinary time and even among bad events: wars and rumours of wars. Most of all, premillennialism is a clarified picture of a future which faithful fundamentalists will assuredly share, in contrast to the failed paradise of Marx's triumphant proletariat or progressivism's promise that things will always keep getting better.

As with beginnings and ends, fundamentalists therefore also know about meanings in the mean time. Specifically, in Muslim, Jewish, and Christian cases alike they see themselves as elect, chosen, and called people with a messianic vision. The ultra-Orthodox in Israel are messianic, but they look for a supernatural revelation of the Messiah and repudiate the secular and Marxist Zionists who founded modern Israel and the liberal statists who have dominated all but some small 'religious' parties ever since. The Shi'ite and Sunni Muslim fundamentalists are sure they know where history is going, and can bear any sacrifice to achieve that to which Allah and the prophet call them.

Theological conversation with the opposed groups in each of the three larger faith communities is seen as futile. What is there to talk about between a member of the Gush Emunim, who will take up arms to defend West Bank settlements or to rebuild the Temple on the Mount where a mosque now blocks the way, and a Reform or Conservative (to say nothing of a secular) Jew, whose sense of election, calling and mission is less certain, or at least less certainly the result of initiating activity through the voice of a revealing God.

6. The consistency and point of oppositionalism

These propaedeutic and substantive philosophy-of-history elements in fundamentalist oppositionalism colour whatever else is at stake in modern theology. If liberal or modernist theologians have proposed it, one must count on fundamentalists to have resisted. This is not to say that in personal life they are all dour and disapproving sorts, or that they cannot tolerate marginal assaults. But fundamentalists have demonstrated an awareness that, in colloquial terms, one can be 'nickeled and dimed to death'. They have recognized better than have many moderates and liberals what the American pundit Walter Lippmann in the 1920s called the 'acids of modernity', and known their corrosive and erosive force. These must not be permitted to infect theological education, confessional expression, philosophical witness, missionary strategy, and the like.

On such terms, one could illustrate, were there space and time, fundamentalist oppositionalism as it treats the issue of the human subject and divine authority. Ever since Friedrich Schleiermacher in Protestant thought and through the work of Bernard Lonergan in *Insight* and the entire corpus of Karl Rahner in Catholicism, there has been an understanding that a first word in scientific inquiry is anthropological; it deals with the human subject. To be sure, some exceptional Protestant movements like the neo-orthodoxy which was associated with Karl Barth were an attempt to counter this main modernist strand, but fundamentalists have rejected Barthianism because it does not begin with testimony to the verbal inerrancy of the original autographs of scripture, and is thus only apparently, to fundamentalists, a deviation from Schleiermacherianism. Indeed, it may be worse than frank modernisms because it lures some from fundamentalism to more open evangelicalisms.

Fundamentalists oppose attention inspired by curiosity about the human subject. It may be of interest to them as psychologists and ordinary citizens, but is given no theological credibility because of human fallenness and fallibility, phenomena which rule out the possibility of authoritative witness to the divine. Instead, there must be absolute authority. For Protestants this comes from the Bible, though, more than is recognized, it is dispensed by authoritative pastors to the faithful, who cannot be expected to find all the literal meanings without help. In Catholicism, pre-Vatican II popes are absolute authorities; the popes who have accepted Vatican II with its putative relativism are thus false popes. In Islam the Qur'an is regarded as a direct utterance from Allah through the prophet by all believers, but fundamentalists especially listen to the voice of the authoritative community leaders for assurance that only one interpretation, a non-interpretation they would say, will be issued.

Given these presuppositional elements there is no need to flesh out the theme with endless illustrations. In Judaism they would deal with rabbinic law or a new Temple. In Islam it would depend upon whether Shi'ite or Sunni makes the theological declarations, and in which country with which contextual polity. In Catholic Christianity there will be contention for the Latin Mass in opposition to the vernacular, as a prime symbolic venture. In Protestantism, 'literal' readings of the doctrine of the virgin birth, the blood atonement and physical resurrection of Christ, accompany claims for the inerrancy of the Bible and the premillennial second coming of Christ.

Rather than spell these out one need only say: assess what moderates, liberals and modernists in a tradition contend and, if you know the texts of the tradition, you can pretty well assume what the fundamentalists will say. They will reject the other options. To speak in such terms seems premature in respect to conversation across party lines, demeaning to the sincere and generous believers who style themselves fundamentalist, and condescending about the sureness of non-fundamentalists. It is intended as anything but that. Instead it takes seriously what all fundamentalists of integrity claim is intrinsic to their integral frameworks. They exist because something they might call modernity came to assault them and they must fight back. They also exist because someone like the modernist came along to urge adaptation to modernity, and the modernist they must resist. Hence the oppositional stance colours all that we associate with all the movements which style themselves fundamentalist or can be styled as fundamentalist-like. The rest is variations on a theme, or footnotes.

Notes

1. Three international, intercultural and inter-religious studies are: Martin E. Marty and R. Scott Appleby, *Fundamentalists Observed*, Chicago 1991; the first of a five-volume study by the Fundamentalism Project of the American Academy of Arts and Sciences, Emile Sahliyeh (ed.), *Religious Resurgence and Politics in the Contemporary World*, Albany, NY 1990; Bruce B. Lawrence, *Defenders of God: The Fundamentalist Revolt Against the Modern Age*, New York 1989. Western Europe

seems to have generated fewer fundamentalisms than most areas of the Christian world; for some European viewpoints in an exercise of comparativism see Martin Riesebrodt, *Fundamentalismus als Patriarchalische Protestbewegung: Amerikanische Protestanten (1910–28) und iranische Schüten (1961–79) im Vergleich*, Tübingen 1990.

2. The best account of American Protestantism is George M. Marsden, *Fundamentalism and American Culture*, New York 1980; Ernest R. Sandeen, *The Roots of Fundamentalism*, Chicago 1970, stresses the fusion of premillennialism and Princeton theology (see below); for an 'up close' view of a congregation see Nancy Tatom Ammerman, *Bible Believers: Fundamentalists in the Modern World*, New Brunswick, NJ 1987. The literature on less developed Catholic fundamentalism is itself less developed, but see the references in and the argument of Thomas F. O'Meara OP, *Fundamentalism: A Catholic Perspective*, New York 1990.

3. Paul Ricoeur, *The Symbolism of Evil*, New York 1967, 347–57, especially 351f.

4. See Karl J. Weintraub, *Visions of Culture*, Chicago 1966, 261, 263.

5. While the book has been criticized because it tends to blur 'evangelicalism' and 'fundamentalism', as is often the case in the United Kingdom, James Barr, *Fundamentalism*, London and Philadelphia 1977, is a helpful elaboration of the biblical views of such movements.

6. For an elaboration, see Kathleen C. Boone, *The Bible Tells Them So: The Discourse of Protestant Fundamentalism*, Albany, NY and London 1989.

7. Isaiah Berlin, *The Crooked Timber of Humanity: Chapters in the History of Ideas*, London and New York 1991; Ernest Gellner, *Contemporary Thought and Politics*, London 1974, 13ff.; John Courtney Murray, *We Hold These Truths*, New York 1960, 23.

8. Helmut R. Wanger, *Alfred Schutz: An Intellectual Biography*, Chicago 1983, 16, 18.

9. Arthur C. Danto, *Analytical Philosophy of History*, Cambridge 1965, Ch. 1, 'Substantive and Analytical Philosophy of History', 1–16.

10. See Timothy P. Weber, *Living in the Shadow of the Second Coming: American Premillennialism, 1875–1982*, enlarged edition, Chicago 1987; Robert G. Clouse (ed.), *The Meaning of the Millennium. Four Views*, Downers Grove, Ill. 1977

What is Fundamentalism Today?
Perspectives in Social Psychology

Geiko Müller-Fahrenholz

1. Fundamentalism – a phenomenon of alienation

If we follow C. Jäggi and D. Krieger, *Fundamentalism. A Phenomenon of the Present*,[1] fundamentalism is a consequence of alienation. The book talks e.g. of 'personal isolation', 'social marginalization', 'losing ethical and cultural roots',[2] or more generally of the loss of historical continuity. Such experiences are matched by a desire for certainty, for 'eternal' truths, for a stable picture of the world. With this desire goes a longing for leader figures who know the right way and therefore have every right to require total subjection.

So fundamentalism is understood as the attempt to overcome a deep existential anxiety and a 'weariness of conflict'.[3] Here psychological categories like 'regresssion' or the Freudian 'Ego/Superego' conceptuality are applied.[4]

These aspects are without doubt appropriate, but they are not sufficient for arriving at a coherent psychological understanding of fundamentalism (it should be noted in passing that Jäggi and Krieger do not make this claim).

I shall go on to add a supplementary perspective which in contrast to the individual psychological perspective might be called 'psycho-historical'. Its aim is to demonstrate the psychological burdens which arise out of social and political revolutions and which therefore have more of a collective origin. Of course I need hardly add that there are also limits to this approach.

2. Fundamentalism and foundations

If one looks at fundamentalism critically, one cannot avoid stressing how significant foundations are for human life. We need foundations in order to be able to live creatively. Without the security and protection of parents and home the healthy development of our emotions and capacities will be restricted. Our physical, intellectual and emotional strength is based on the foundations of love, care and trust.

This also holds in a trans-personal sense. Communities, clans and peoples need their history, i.e. their traditions, rites and cults, in order to be able to exist creatively and in a balanced way and to look to the future.

But there is yet a further dimension. A Chinese proverb says, 'States and governments come and go, but the mountains remain.' This is an expression of confidence in the stability of earth and time. Whatever may happen to us human beings and our peoples, earth and time remain. This is expressed in an archaic way in the blessing on Noah: 'While the earth remains, seedtime and harvest, cold and heat, summer and winter, day and night, shall not cease' (Gen. 8.22).

This fundamental confidence is the most original way in which we human beings cope with the most disquieting problem of our existence, namely our mortality. Although our lives as individuals and collective have their time, time itself is without time. 'Life goes on', people say, often after having been at the graveside, and the statement is an expression of primal confidence in the fundamental reliability of existence.

Along with this also goes confidence in the reliability of the future as a time to come. Even if our own particular future may be uncertain, there must be no doubt about the future itself. This basic confidence in the eternal rhythm of day and night, summer and winter, is essential as a compensation to the constant endangering of our lives.

Creative life in all its forms develops on the basis of this confidence in earth and time. Creativity is identity in transition, as an appropriation of the past and its transformation into something new. Societies, cultures and religions, in short all living systems, show their life precisely by being capable of this appropriation and transformation.

But what happens if this fundamental confidence in earth and time is lost? If a traumatic process obscures the creative appropriation of the past and blocks the transformation of what has been inherited into an open future? Wherever such collapses in appropriation and transformation take place, i.e. where there is the 'end of a world' without a new order becoming visible, fundamentalist reactions emerge. So we can understand fundamentalism as pathological reactions to the experiences of the end of a world. Here are four examples.

3. Fundamentalism as the experience of the end of a world.

(a) Islamic fundamentalism

Arab-Islamic fundamentalism is understandable only in a historic perspective. Four factors in particular must be indicated here.

1. The memory of the Arab-Islamic world empire which in its heyday was superior to all other peoples, above all European and Christian peoples. Even today the collapse of this world empire is a trauma.

However, even more hurtful was and is, 2. the fact that the European people in particular, above all England and France, and in our century the USA, were able to become colonial lords over the Arab and Islamic world. The Gulf War at the beginning of 1991 with its shaming effectiveness is just the last link, for the moment, in a long chain of humiliations.

3. Furthermore, Islam understands itself as the divinely-appointed religious and political order for the whole world. So it entered history as a religion of victors. If 'unbelievers' are now robbing this faith of its power, traumatic confusions in the understanding of faith are inevitable.

4. Finally, as yet Islam has found no way of tackling creatively the phenomenon of modernity, especially the phenomenon of secularity. Although in its heyday it was able to appropriate the literary, scientific and technical achievements of the peoples in its sphere of influence and transform them into a world culture, it failed at the second stage of appropriating the modern civilization which came into being in Europe, even though it has its roots in the Arab heritage. It can understand that civilization only as a threat, as a heightening of what is already an accumulation of collective injuries.

So we can speak of the traumatic experience of the 'end of a world' which underlies Islamic fundamentalism. This experience prevents the working out of a renewed Arab-Islamic understanding of faith and self-understanding.

(b) North American fundamentalism

A fundamentalism has established itself on the conservative wing of North American Protestantism which reflects quite a different experience of the 'end of a world'. Whereas 'classical' fundamentalism in the United States at the beginning of this century had markedly anti-modernistic features – an aspect which still continues to have an influence, for example among the 'moral majority' – fundamentalism today has another theme, namely the question of the end of history.

An apocalyptic feeling about the world is manifest in many statements by preachers of the Electronic Church. According to them, history is to be understood simply as the eschatological battle between Christ and the Antichrist.[5] These eschatological scenarios, which are taken from apocalyptic literature before and after the birth of Christ, need not be described here. What is of interest to us is the question how it can be that such apocalyptic fantasies can find so great an echo in the most powerful country on earth.

My conjecture is that many people in the USA find the present situation of the world extremely confusing. Furthermore, they experience the complexity and arbitrariness of the events which encounter them in a constant bombardment from the mass media as a diffuse overloading of their psychological capacities. The news of nuclear infernos possible at any time and of ecological catastrophes have undermined their confidence in time.

Now indeed the most fundamental demand of our time is that of coming to terms with the fact that with the beginning of the nuclear age all future time has taken on an eschatological character. The unprecedented power of human beings, who if they cannot make their future can at least destroy it, represents a captivity hitherto unknown.

Apocalyptic fundamentalism in the USA is the perpetuation of this challenge. The unprecedented power of human beings over the future of history is rejected. Its place is taken by Christ and Antichrist as the real subjects of history. All human beings and powers are now reduced to being servants in the super-terrestrial struggle for power, and this brings with it an enormous shedding of the burden of political responsibility. So this modern apocalyptic fundamentalism reflects a widespread capitulation to the unprecedented power and responsibility of human beings in the nuclear age – it is a syndrome of overloading which presumably just took place earlier in the USA than in other countries.

(c) Fundamentalism in Latin America

The striking growth of the so-called 'fundamentalist sects' in Central and South America is often attributed to the intensive missionary work of North American fundamentalists. However, in my view that is not the explanation of their great success. Rather, I assume that here too one can talk of the end of a world, to which the fundamentalist preaching offers an answer.

It is often overlooked that the last thirty years there have seen not only far-reaching economic impoverishment but with it also a disintegration of the traditional rural culture. The migration into the mega-slums of the cities has already led to deculturation and alienation. This is as it were intensified to the point of addiction by the massive invasion of the mass media shaped by the West, which suggest illusory pictures of a beautiful life alien to reality. The familiar world has come to an end, life seems caught in a chaotic spiral downwards in which nothing is reliable any longer.

In this situation of economic and social impoverishment and emotional disturbance, the fundamentalist message offers a welcome refuge. Structurally, the message is like the apocalyptic message from the USA. Here too the real agents are Christ and Antichrist, but the poor are no longer just the nameless victims. Rather, by conversion and sanctification they are promised a new dignity, a new community and eternal life.

(d) Institutional fundamentalism

Finally, it should be pointed out here that institutions, hierarchies and elites, too, can react in a fundamentalistic way, if the complexity of the situation gets too much for them. Thus Stalinism was a fundamentalism, and the Reagan and Bush administrations also react in a fundamentalist way to world situations which have become uncontrollable. But the present-day policy of the Vatican is also a characteristic example.

The Second Vatican Council represents a large-scale attempt to redefine the message and ethos of the Catholic church world-wide under modern conditions: it is a typical process of appropriation and transformation. As could have been foreseen, in various regions of this world church it tested the system to breaking point because the processes initiated by the council had to be received by the faithful and their local hierarchies.

This was certainly a kind of 'end of the world', not least for the Vatican authorities and the pope. Thus it is becoming more and more evident that the innovatory risk of the Council is seen as a danger. And by every possible means attempts are being made to restore the familiar Catholic world. Clearly this process is having increasingly anachronistic and self-destructive consequences: one need only think of the problems of birth control and the priesthood.

4. The pathology of experiences of the end of the world

I have attempted by means of four examples to demonstrate that there are different experiences of the end of a world and therefore different forms of fundamentalist reaction. Any 'end of the world' must seem like an incursion of chaos which makes the working out of new orders impossible and provokes experiences of helplessness. It seems to me that this helplessness is the element which is characteristic of all fundamentalists, despite all the differences. However, this is a helplessness which cannot concede that it is helpless.

Therefore by absolutizing fundamentals it seeks a new power – and is indifferent to whether this power is rooted in the past (e.g. the great Arab empire) or the future (the kingdom of God). It is in the nature of this borrowed power that, depending on the nature of the opponents, it can be used aggressively, violently or in a hostile way, just as it can prove protective and provide an authoritarian security for those under its wing.

It is in the nature of borrowed power to use certain instruments from a world which it otherwise scorns. These may be technical means, techniques of academic research, media, advertising strategies, etc. This selective, instrumental use of rationality and modernity can give fundamentalist presentations as it were a partial logic and coherence of argument, and also considerable political influence. However, the power which is borrowed cannot fill the gap occupied by the inner horror that has come about through a loss of confidence in earth and time. So this vacuum remains as an abyss of doubt and must constantly be assuaged.

That explains the totalism of fundamentalist systems, which expresses itself in different ways. As traditionalism in the sphere of doctrine it ensures that there is no room for criticism of the basic texts and a systematic discussion of the structure of faith. As authoritarianism it prevents the development and discussion of alternatives in the sector of social organization. As fanaticism it mobilizes control among believers to the point of brainwashing potential deviants and implements defensive or offensive strategies against opponents.

So this totalism explains why fundamentalist groups often engage in socially disruptive action and are either reserved about or opposed to efforts at social and political reform.

We can follow Robert J. Lifton and take these psycho-historical reflections one stage further. Lifton regards fundamentalism as a particular expression of 'numbing' which can come about under the stress of circumstances which have been intolerable.[6] This disturbance expresses itself as a partial lack of feeling and a limited perception of reality.

This helps us to understand better attitudes in fundamentalist systems which seem extreme, like the extreme coldness of feeling in the Armageddon fantasies of apocalyptic fundamentalists; the 'Satanizing' of the West, especially the USA, during the Islamic revolution (a revolution backwards) under Ayatollah Khomeini; and the almost hermetic political blindness of fundamentalist groups in Central America.

Lifton also points out that a certain psychological disposition is needed for a person to adopt fundamentalist positions. He distinguishes the Protean type from the 'holdfast' type.[7] Proteus, the ancient God of the waves, constantly adopts new forms, whereas the mythological figure of the 'holdfast' is incapable of movement and seeks to grip on to everything. Lifton shows that under the pressure of deadly threats many people react in a 'Protean' way, i.e. are interested in everything and nothing without sustaining any commitment. By contrast, the 'holdfast' type shows the opposite disposition and embraces a particular view of reality, elevating it to become an 'eternal' truth and defending it to the last breath. Thus holdfast individuals or communities are inclined to adopt fundamentalist positions. The consequences are a lack of capacity for innovation and change, and rigidity and hardness.

5. Can fundamentalism be overcome?

I have described fundamentalist systems as pathological phenomena arising out of profound disturbances. As our day is seeing an extraordinarily rapid change of epoch which involves all cultures and societies, fundamentalist reactions are not surprising. As I have already said, today's global crisis puts our basic confidence and power of transformation to a severe test.

So the question of overcoming fundamentalism lies more within the framework of the question 'How can and should a fundamental trust be preserved or re-formed under conditions of constant finitude and increasing impoverishment?'

Of course this question goes far beyond the framework of these psycho-historical reflections. But I should at least indicate the direction in which I would look for the beginning of an answer.

If fundamentalism is an expression of collective disturbance and hardening, any attempt to overcome it must begin with empathy and sensitivity. Fundamentalism cannot be fought against.

Moreover, a truly ecumenical effort is called for from all authorities concerned with a meaningful life, i.e. above all the world religions, to develop new spiritual orientations which can offer human beings life and trust in the midst of a stream of history which threatens to knock them off their feet. The memory of humankind is rich in images and symbols of the sanctity and worth of all life, or responsibility for justice, joy and fullness of life (*shalom*). Where it proves possible to renew the supportive energies of these traditions and above all build up communities which can sustain and create trust, it may also prove possible to overcome, or better to heal, fundamentalism.

Translated by John Bowden

Notes

1. C. Jäggi and D. Krieger, *Fundamentalismus. Ein Phänomen der Gegenwart*, Zurich 1991. In my view this is the most comprehensive account of the problem. In this context cf. 'Psychische Aspekte fundamentalistischer Haltungen', 25ff.
2. Ibid., 25.
3. Ibid., 31.
4. Ibid., 27.

5. Cf. Hal Lindsay, *The Late Great Planet Earth*, Toronto and New York [36] 1981. The publishers point out that 15 million copies are already in circulation. That is an illuminating indication of the attraction and dissemination of this type of fundamentalism.

6. Cf. R. J. Lifton, *The Life of the Self. Toward a New Psychology*, New York 1963; id., *Indefensible Weapons. The Political and Psychological Case against Nuclearism* (with R. Falk), New York 1982; id., *The Future of Immortality*, New York 1987. Lifton gives the following definition of numbing: 'Psychic numbing is a general category of diminished capacity or inclination to feel. Psychic numbing involves an interruption in psychic action – in the continuous creation and re-creation of images and forms that constitute the symbolizing or "formative process" characteristic of human life. Psychic numbing varies greatly in degree, from everyday blocking of excessive stimuli to extreme manifestations in response to death-saturated environments,' in id., *The Nazi Doctors. Medical Killing and the Psychology of Genocide*, New York 1986, 442.

7. Id., *The Future of Immortality* (n. 6), 17ff.

Fundamentalism, Dogmatism, Fanaticism: Psychiatric perspectives

Günter Hole

Here I shall be analysing the three terms fundamentalism, dogmatism and fanaticism to establish their different meanings and levels. Each relates to a different level not only of motives and attitudes, but also of psycho-dynamic processes. To begin with, I shall mention what is common to all three attitudes and perspectives, namely that the people with whom we shall be concerned here have such total and unassailable aims and faith that they can no longer accept other convictions and attitudes alongside their own. This is where the consensus lies, and it is this which makes up the opposite pole to pluralism.

1. The characteristic features

If we analyse fundamentalist, dogmatic and even more fanatical attitudes more closely, we encounter three particularly striking principles, though with differing focal points. The first is consistency, i.e. consistency both in forming an idea and acting upon it. The second, which applies above all to fundamentalism and fanaticism, is that these modes of thought, attitudes and systems are characterized by a special simplicity, and perspectives which differentiate to a greater degree are largely excluded. The third principle, which distinguishes the dogmatic attitude above all, is clarity of statement, and thus also the establishment of interpretations and doctrinal structures. It is the combination of these three factors which makes such attitudes so enormously effective in the world, and gives the 'movements' characterized by them such impetus in human social life. This applies above all when the groups or individuals in question have appropriate means of power at their disposal.

After these general comments on the characteristics and above all the common features of fundamentalist, dogmatic and fanatical attitudes, I shall now go on to differentiate and define the individual terms and their perspectives. However, we shall not be concerned here with precise, abstract definitions, but rather with a point-by-point description of the essential characteristics in so far as they seem important for further understanding. I understand the three terms as follows:

Fundamentalism

An attitude to a basic value or basic idea which must be protected in a perfectionist way; in addition, there is an anxiety about the loss of this value through compromise.

Characteristic of this is a need for:
– Anchoring;
– Clear identification;
– Perfectionism;
– Simplicity.

Dogmatism

The construction of a system around a value or an attitude and the protection of it by argument; this includes the importance of the explication of this attitude as doctrine, and the precise demarcation of it from other spheres of value and thought.

Characteristic of this is a need for:
– Clarity;
– Norms;
– Authority;
– Certainty.

Fanaticism

Abnormal intensity in the pursuit and implementation of one attitude or idea with a special value; here there is a lack of capacity for self-criticism and a projective defence against all contrary views.

Characteristic of this is a need for:
– Confirmation of the self;
– Aggressive assertion;
– Absolute validity;
– Consistency.

As we know, such attitudes have very varied social effects. Certainly there are also purely personal fundamentalist and fanatical patterns in lives which do not castigate others (e.g. in the case of food fanatics, silent ascetic or inventive types – to which we shall be returning in due course). But as soon as the framework of action and the sphere of power goes beyond the individual person, it always has the enormous effect on other systems and groups which I have already mentioned. This already begins in the family, in the presentation of key values by a parent or another member of the family – still expressed in positive terms. This can very quickly lead to a personal domination, as often also happens above all in a partnership in which one individual is always expressing the opinions and giving the directions. In extreme cases this leads to real family tyranny, with the type of family tyrant who presents his or her own values, ideas and needs to everyone else and also has the power to impose them, usually by sheer force of personality. Such attitudes and aims have even more fatal effects when the means of power, especially also the effect of suggestions and the development of resonances, are systematically incorporated into a social group, because then they have an essentially wider scope. For such giving of values, setting of aims and demarcation can of course run quite contrary to the values and aims of other members in a social environment. If such principles, or individuals with such attitudes, then finally exert influence in senior social positions – in the state, church, associations, radical groups – the situation can not only become extremely oppressive but also result in a real lack of freedom for those with other views. Here what had already been given in the 'claim to absoluteness' has then already been achieved. The establishment of simple, radical goals can then lead with utter consistency to the real exclusion and elimination of those who think otherwise. There are plenty of terrifying instances of this.

2. Fundamentalist ideas as a problem for everyone

Described in this way, it might seem that the problem of fundamentalism and fanaticism is ultimately a problem of clearly definable people or systems who are to be evaluated in negative terms, e.g. the fanatic, the family tyrant, the concentration camp guard, the Inquisition, the Third Reich, antisemitism, terrorists, the youth sects. In this way we could make things very easy for ourselves: conveniently mark out the whole topic and simply assign it to the theme of 'evil in the world'. If we did that, we would then once again have successfully bracketted this evil off from ourselves in a personal or systemic way and pushed it off somewhere else.

But we ourselves are equally the subject of this theme. We need only attempt to take a look at ourselves, and systematic experience of ourselves will confirm the fact further: all of us have such tendencies towards fundamentalist attitudes within us – even more so if we are very fascinated with ideal values, contents of faith and imperatives of perfection, as in the Christian sphere. Moreover, it is very easy for hidden fanatical elements which many of us also carry around within us to pop out, at least as indications of a proneness to this direction. For just as iron filings in a magnetic field arrange themselves in accordance with this magnetic field, so evidently particular elements in our character are prepared to arrange themselves in accordance with a stronger field of force created by values and aims.

This is the only way in which we can understand the phenomenon of the fellow-traveller, the person who shares the convictions of, or is a hanger-on in, an extremist political or religious system. Individuals can only be genuine fellow-travellers if there is something in them that goes along with the system, if they have some resonance with it, if some part of them are infected and can be pushed in a particular direction. So this theme is a theme for all of us, and not just about 'evil persons'. Nor are we concerned here simply with the state of part of the world as something which can be demarcated and split off from us; rather, we are quite vitally concerned with the dynamics of our own inner life, with what is taking place at the highest levels of our personalities. The task facing us includes the psychological analysis of both fanatical systems and fanatical personalities on the one hand and our own inner world on the other.

We have to train ourselves to perceive clearly and accept how far we ourselves bear within ourselves aspects and tendencies of a fundamentalist or fanatical kind, especially the tendency also to arrange our world of individual and collective values in accordance with a quite specific individual value. I began by mentioning such values, some of which have a high status. Suppose we take, for example, a person with a very compulsive structure, for whom order represents a very high value. With this order, with this principle of order, such a person can not only tyrannize a whole family, but, given the possibility, can go even further and also tyrannize other individuals. Here indeed we speak directly of someone who is a 'fanatic for order'. This proneness often results in even the complex individual value systems to which a person is brought up being arranged around a particular individual value, in this case that of order. We speak in an analogous way of e.g. a 'fanatic for justice', a 'fanatic for purity', a 'racial fanatic' or even a 'religious fanatic'.

What is striking, and to that degree also particularly alarming, in such cases is that highly-prized values are involved in them. Accordingly, those concerned also have no awareness of being in the wrong; on the contrary, subjectively they are fighting for what is good and right. An important process is clearly at work here, namely that even a differentiated superego – to use a psychological language – can be ideologically directed or co-ordinated by shifting to lower levels other values which previously had the same status. That is the only way in which we can understand how – when he has the opportunity and at the same time also the justification – an upright, average citizen can actually live out fanatical or sadistic traits, for example as a concentration-camp guard. This is not because in principle he is a more evil person than others, but because by being co-ordinated at the level of the superego, these traits are released in him. For me, this proneness to ideology of our highest regulative values, and therefore of the superego or the conscience – I mention both together in this case, though they are two different authorities in the individual – is one of the most oppressive of phenomena. It is very closely connected with our high esteem for the ideal and the perfect, and far too little work has been done on it, particularly in the Christian spheres. At any rate, the human capacity for enthusiasm, our capacity for letting ourselves be carried away, means not only the possibility of high flights but also the possibility of a deep fall into the inhuman. And that our structure of values can be infected in particular by explicit ideal values in this way raises particularly explosive questions about our Christian imperatives.

Given all that I have said, we urgently need better models for explaining and understanding these phenomena. They must be capable of being popularized with the aim of overcoming or preventing the destructive development of fanatical traits in our personalities. However, only a few people can cope with the development of clearer awareness at this level, and for that a good deal of prior experience of introspection is needed. Still, a model for understanding and fairly clear contours emerge from the description and discussion of typical 'fanatical personalities', and from that important psychological processes can also be transferred to the average psyche. The 'fanatical personalities' embody extreme expressions, to some degree exemplary forms, of the fanatic, and also shed some light on the background to fundamentalist and dogmatic attitudes in different spheres of life and faith.

3. Fanaticism as personality structure

First of all some interesting aspects of the history of the term. It is illuminating and important for our subject that the word 'fanaticism' is derived from the religious sphere. It is directly connected with the root *fas* or *fes*, which means 'religious act': the 'fanatic' was the person who rushed around the *fanum*, the holy place; the reference was probably also to ecstasy. Very soon the term 'fanatic' was applied to anyone who was seized by the divine *furor*, the divine fire. In early Christianity all pagan priests and cultic servants then came to be called *fanatici*, the fanatical then already being projected on to an alien group.

This significance of demarcation in the religious sphere was then preserved in the future. In the Reformation the *fanatici* were the religious enthusiasts and sectarians – of course from the perspective of the Reformers – while on the other hand 'fanaticism' applied from the Catholic side to Protestantism itself. Melanchthon turned this round again and made the charge of fanaticism against the early church, interestingly above all with a reference to celibacy. Around 1700 the best way of making a religious movement look ridiculous was to be able to demonstrate that it was fanatical. So the reference to fanaticism was an important and usable weapon. Accordingly, in the French Revolution, Reason, which was highly stylized, was seen especially as the annihilation of fanaticism; however, after a short time the term was reversed once again and applied to the effects of the French Revolution itself, to the Jacobins, Robespierre, etc. Only for perhaps 200 years have people stopped prescribing qualifications for the term fanaticism in terms of content and have come to see it as primarily a problem of intensity of attitudes and modes of action, quite independent of content.

In the system of psychiatry, fanaticism has long been assigned a particular place as a particular type of personality: there are variants ranging from 'normal' to 'abnormal'. Here 'abnormal' is primarily value-neutral and means deviation from the norm, the average. Whether sickness is also a factor here does not follow from this statistical statement, but from possible additional symptoms, i.e. as the result of a particular act of diagnosis. Certainly, sometimes fanatical modes of behaviour follow from genuine psychological illness, but this need not concern us here now. The main problem of 'fanaticism' is not one of disease but one of typical personality-structures. It is very important to note this. Thus for example there are personalities which are abnormally explosive or abnormally volatile or abnormally unemotional without this necessarily having to be a symptom of illness. Rather, these are primarily simple species and variations of nature, just as there are also variations at all biological levels. The so-called fanatical personalities may be looked on in an analogous way. The other important question, how such traits emerge in the first place, i.e. how much of them is already innate and how much is caused by the environment, above all by development in early childhood and general socialization, is very difficult to answer. This problem underlies all the old disputes between psychopathy and character neurosis, which need not concern us further here.

Thus typically fanatical personalities are marked out by quite specific abnormal traits. It is the extreme variants of such personalities in particular which have been called 'fanatical psychopaths', thus bringing this term 'psychopathy' generally into disrepute. In what follows I shall simply speak of 'abnormal personalities', pointing out that the extreme variants among them are those who as a result of their abnormal characteristics either suffer themselves or make those around them suffer. The type of the fanatical personality belongs to the latter group, and is the one which causes serious problems: such people do not themselves suffer as a result of their characteristics (as do e.g. depressives or the unemotional); rather the ones who suffer are those around them, and they do so quite enormously – at best with the exception of the fanatic's own followers. Moreover, those not under pressure from suffering are also not prepared to change their behaviour – why should they? In therapy, too, continuous work can be done only on the basis of such a pressure of suffering. Furthermore, those who do not suffer do not go in search of help. So the fanatics never come to therapy of their own accord; at best they are compelled to do so by pressure from outside, and then they have no motivation for therapy. On the contrary, they are simply concerned to carry through their own attitudes and aims consistently, and if they have the power, that is what they will do. So against such people – and this is already an important anticipation of the question how far tolerance here is possible – the only course is to engage in clear counter-actions from outside: demarcation, legal measures or open combat. It is almost always vain to attempt to convince fanatics, and we shall have to work out more clearly why.

In his book *Geniale Menschen*, Ernst Kretschmer has given a very vivid description of the way in which we must imagine the influence of such abnormal personalities being exercised on society as a whole. He compares this with the working of bacilli in the organism:

> If the spiritual temperature of an age is balanced and the social organism sound, the abnormal swarm helplessly among the mass of healthy people without much effect. But if there is a sore point anywhere, if the air is stifling or filled with tension, if something is foul and rotten, the bacilli immediately become virulent, capable of attack, penetrate everywhere and inflame the whole of the healthy mass of people and cause it to ferment . . . The major fanatics, the prophets and enthusiasts, like the small crooks and criminals, are always there and the air is full of them; but it is only when the spirit of an age gets overheated that they can beget war, revolution and spiritual mass movements. One could rightly say that the psychopaths are always there. But in cool times we diagnose them and in hot times they dominate us.

With this last statement, which quotation has made famous, Kretschmer has identified the explosive social and political-psychological problem which also forms the background to our theme. It needs a special thorough analysis of its own.

4. Phenomenology of the fanatical type

First, what is the phenomenology of the fanatical type? What are its basic characteristics? Taking up the general characteristics that I already mentioned at the beginning, which also apply to fundamentalist and dogmatic attitudes (namely a striving for consistency, simplicity and clarity), I would go on to draw the picture on these lines. What is characteristic is the fact of being possessed with one idea or attitude of faith which allows no other possibility beside it. Furthermore, for those concerned, this idea has to be marked out or implemented sharply if they are not to feel restricted. This is in turn connected with the fact that here we have the expression of a fundamental 'either-or' attitude as a structural part of the personality. Finally, we must note that there is such certainty over this idea or attitude that those who have it cannot be shaken. This sometimes already goes some way towards being a delusion, although as a rule there are clear psychiatric bounds to a real delusion. Delusion itself is a phenomenon of sickness, whereas this kind of certainty and unshakability in the fanatical type is a personality element. Similarly, there is also a clear distinction between delusion and belief (which, however, we cannot go into here). That generally the psychology of the saints overlaps in many respects with the psychology of fanatics, particularly in the characteristics I have mentioned, is obvious. The biographies of the saints are treasure troves for living expressions of many elements of fanaticism, but these elements are also often compensated for by characteristics of quite a different kind which emerge at the same time. Here the criterion lies in the evaluation of a life as a whole, but there are also dangers here for any judgment by the church, in that extremism and rigorism can be regarded as signs of special perfection.

Of course, attempts have been made to produce a differentiated typology for fanatical personalities. I want to be brief on this point, and simply refer to some details which are also important for our theme. First of all a distinction is made between the so-called active, expansive fanatics and the so-called silent or dull fanatics.

Active and expansive fanatics usually show the following traits: a strong drive and biologically strong activity generally, a high need of status or a quest for status, and sometimes also what is termed a lack of emotion, i.e. a lack of those emotional forces which represent even a small capacity to be bound to social values and other people. Thus typical fanatical personalities are unable to make human ties, and this is a very important point. The active, expansive fanatics also include the so-called 'personal fanatics', who make an enormous aggressive impact on their social environment usually because of a personal insult or slight which can be over a relatively small matter. This is the type depicted by Michael Kohlhaas, who because of a petty conflict over two horses finally becomes an incendiary and a troublemaker; as a classic 'fanatic for justice' he feels that he is a kind of divine avenger and commits much injustice in the name of the law. He has to carry on this battle in which the ultimate concern is simply to 'get his rights', because only in that way can supposed justice in the legal sense be restored. I deliberately say 'has to', since behind this there is an inner compulsion – the compulsion to be a consistent personality. Here we experience consistency quite clearly as a destructive consistency, and this type of basic attitude can be found quite often in an everyday form. But we must always keep in mind how highly this basic characteristic of being consistent is also rated in our evaluations, and what high praise it can be for us to say that a person is consistent. Later I shall be speaking of this oppressive juxtaposition in further detail.

In addition to these active, expansive fanatics there is also the type of the silent fanatic which I have already mentioned, also somewhat mistakenly described as the dull fanatic. Such people cherish an unshakable conviction all their lives in silent stubbornness, and also live it out consistently. Often the special content of this conviction cannot be discovered, and it can prove quite reasonable. This is the category to which certain fanatical opponents of vaccination, vegetarians and inventive types belong, and also some members of sects. Here we also speak of an 'overrated' idea, to the extent that this idea takes exclusive possession of a person's whole existence. We can detect quite a few 'silent' fanatics among the heretics in church history and also among the members of present-day sects and other extremist groups. These are not the most militant leaders of such groups, but followers who gather in this catchment area and so can express their silent fanatical traits. They do not make a great stir, nor are they dangerous, but in terms of psychodynamics they certainly belong to this type. When it comes to external conflict, these people are equally unbending and ready to resist, with all the suffering which that may involve. There are many examples of this kind.

However, most fanatics about ideas are expansive militants, i.e. those who can be described as activists. They are the ones who really make an effect on society, and they do so principally on the basis of the character defects which they also have. Weitbrecht says of them – and this is to some degree a continuation of the statement from Kretschmer quoted above:

The most dangerous of these types are people lacking emotion and values to bind them other than those which they themselves make, with a view to their own success . . . It is only a tiny chance of birth and circumstances that some of the 'great men' of history did not become highly distinctive criminals.

This way of putting it is very dramatic and may sound exaggerated, but the direction in which it points is certainly correct.

5. Schizoid, paranoid and hysterical characteristics

As I have already said, there are also reciprocal relationships and links with other personality characteristics which lead to marked modes of behaviour, particularly when these characteristics are of a typically neurotic nature. Mention should be made here especially of the so-called schizoid personality structure. Here Rudin has pointed in particular to the marked 'psychological rigidity in thinking and imagining', and also the striking 'abruptness of effect' and the total 'identification with the idea' to which such a person is then indissolubly bound to the bitter end. Petrilowitsch stressed above all the close reciprocal relationship with paranoid personalities, who similarly belong to the schizoid type. These are people who have a marked tendency always to apply the words and actions of other people to themselves, who are thus excessively mistrustful and as a result project their own fears on the environment. According to Petrilowitsch and others, the common feature of such people is an abnormal capacity to persist in their own convictions, the narrowing of their field of vision and the blind passion with which they pursue such convictions, and their inability to compromise. These are above all the typical *terribles simplificateurs*, to whom the views of others are interesting only to the degree that they confirm their own. On top of this there is also a false estimation or overestimation of their own capacities, along with an inability to engage in self-criticism. Moreover, sooner or later most fanatics show paranoid traits; they thus live by incorrigible projections and see any resistance from the environment only as the enemy or as an evil which has to be fought against all the more vigorously. In his book *Körperbau und Charakter*, Kretschmer speaks succinctly of the 'schizothymic triad', idealism, fanaticism and despotism. This triad can be perceived as clearly in such prominent religious minds as Calvin and Savonarola as in Robespierre as a political leader.

Among the persons concerned, combinations of a fanatical nature with compulsive traits lead above all to a feeling of strong inner compulsion, which as a result of a strong identification with particular ideas is then often experienced as a special 'mission'. Moreover, such persons tend particularly to be fixated on rigid formulae, faithfulness to the letter and the formulation of a doctrine. This is the link with dogmatism, which generally stems from the needs of compulsive natures; this also makes clear the one-sidedness and danger of dogmatic thought. Moreover compulsive fanatics, on the basis of the stimuli held off in this structure, tend in particular to live out aggressive impulses, especially in a cruel, sadistic way – which also includes pious mercilessness.

Typical hysterical traits emerge in connection with basic fanatical structures, above all in the tendency to unrestrained outbursts of feeling, to allow oneself to give way to momentary fanatical actions and commands. The hysterical element consists in a little-developed sense of the ego and the self, and the experiencing of oneself in a particular role, before an environment which is impressed by it, heightens such a feeling. Therefore on the other hand hysterical fanatics can also exercise a special fascination, and this is often the characteristic which sparks off a whole movement and its followers, whose capacity for enthusiasm, readiness to be identified with it, and openness to being infected by fanaticism form the breeding ground. This is the only way in which we can arrive at some sort of understanding of Hitler and the effect he had: the characteristics of a combined fanatical and hysterical structure are unmistakable in him, as is clear above all from the reports of those closest to him.

6. The psychodynamics of the fanatical personality

Following on from this typological differentation I must now say something about the psychodynamics of personalities with a fanatical structure. The question here is what is really taking place in the inner play of psychological forces. These processes also apply to a lesser degree to the hidden traits and possibilites which many of us carry around within ourselves, as I already mentioned at the beginning. The majority of people with a fanatical attitude show wide-ranging problems in the sphere of self-esteem. This lack of self-esteem is intolerable, so such people are also completely without humour. Humour presupposes the capacity to put oneself in question in a relaxed and cheerful way; by contrast, those who must be scrupulously careful not to be irritated at any point, so that their sense of inferiority does not appear, cannot open themselves even to sympathetic criticism. Typical fanatics are therefore in 'dead earnest' and at the same time have a strong personal sensitivity and vulnerability. Often there is a contrast here to individuals' failures and inadequacies in their own quite personal life and experience, specifically in the private sphere. However, conversely, among fanatics there are also those who simply by nature have a very good or already heightened sense of self-esteem; they have the feeling that they are the ones who are basically all right, without needing any compensatory process.

Still, above all it is also important that these people are usually incapable of empathy with others: this lack explains a great deal in the behaviour of fanatics. For if I can understand other people, then I can also understand other estimations of values and then I can also allow something like that to exist, i.e. I can be tolerant. Thus tolerance presupposes a capacity for empathy for other people and other systems. Furthermore, fanatics are very strongly marked by a general inability to be flexible, by their rigid adherence to habits, their incapacity to change, their rigidity in the emotional sphere, which I have already mentioned. These personalities are particularly deficient in this emotional sphere, so far as it also relates above to social life, ties to other people.

Indeed it has always been striking that when it comes to the structural characteristics of fanaticism, men are by far in the majority. There are far fewer fanatical women in this sense, and if there are, they stand out especially for their 'unfeminine' characteristics. However, we cannot discuss here how much is a matter of heredity and how much is conditioned by education and social processes.

A further central point in the psychodynamics of fanatical personalities consists in the strikingly 'rigid identification with an absolute ideal', as Schmidbauer puts it; this ideal, or more precisely the idealized object, here 'is experienced as a part of a person's own self'. Just as in infatuation and in love we transform part of our own ego or self to another person, so here too it is transferred to and invested in an idea. In this way, of course, a person's own destiny is also bound up to death and destruction with the destiny of this idea.

In the last resort we keep coming up against the fact that a basically fanatical disposition is connected with compensation for a personal defect. Here Rudin speaks directly of 'intensity as compensation'. And indeed it is striking that most of the time a quite specific deficiency has to be compensated for, namely doubt as to the validity of the idea put forward. If a person takes a particular direction, then of course voices are also raised against him or her. Usually a person can tolerate this. Here, however, these opposing inner voices are compensated for by a fanatical high stylization of the idea itself. C. G. Jung once said that fanaticism was the 'brother of doubt': i.e., someone who somewhere harbours secret doubts can compensate for them by embracing his idea even more loudly and intensely, in the sense of 'now even more'.

This process is also important in the psychology of religion generally, because such over-compensations by a loud confession to oneself and others can also be found in the life of faith. On the one hand we know people who believe quite naturally, simply and firmly, on the basis of their primal trust. And then there are zealots in faith who already in hectoring language and with overflowing need seek to convince others absolutely, are active in mission, and manifestly cannot relax. This can be a sign that here someone is having to suppress doubt in the faith. Such people cannot bear the emergence of doubt, though the normal psychology of religion teaches us that doubt goes along with faith – otherwise we would be closed and completed systems. But in fanatical people these doubts strike so deeply into their own self-esteem that they have to be vigorously repudiated and fought against – among others, i.e. projectively.

In this connection, finally, we come up against the question whether there is such a thing as the 'ideological personality'. What is meant by this is the sort of person who naturally lives mainly by an idea and by abstract idealistic goals because he or she cannot live spontaneously by the fullness of life and the value of human ties. We must answer this question in the affirmative, and from the traits described so far, the psychological contours of the type emerge very vividly: we encounter them not only as fanatical extremes but very often in the form of the fundamentalist theoretician, the idealistic intellectual and the dogmatist who is concerned for law and 'pure doctrine'. The normative type of this 'ideological personality' corresponds, to use Kretschmer's terminology, not so much to the emotional pycnomorph, but more to the schizothymic, leptosome person with abrupt changes of emotion. For such a person, intimacy and ties to other people presents a problem which is hard to cope with; such people therefore feel happier on the level of ideas, ideals and theoretical connections. So truth or justice have a higher status among ethical values here than love or personal ties. Of course this is an over-simplistic way of putting things, far less can it provide any moral assessment. But it may have become clear how important are the perspectives which arise from all this.

Translated by John Bowden

Bibliography

Kretschmer, E., *Körperbau und Character*, Berlin [20]1951, quotation 329.
id., *Geniale Menschen*, Berlin [5]1958, quotation 19f.
Marquard, O., 'Über die Unvermeidlichkeit der Geisteswissenschaften', in *Uni Ulm intern* 16, 1986, 127/8, 18–23
Petrilowitsch, N., *Abnorme Persönlichkeiten*, Basel [2]1964, quotation 117
Popper, K. E, *Unended Quest*, London 1986
Rudin, I., *Fanatismus*, Olten [2]1975, quotations 64, 66, 164, 166, 172
Schmidbauer, W., *Alles oder nichts. Über die Destruktivität von Idealen*, Hamburg 1980, 183

Schneider, K., *Klinische Psychopathologie: Psychopathische Persönlich-keiten*, Stuttgart [5]1959, 15–37

Spaemann, R., 'Fanatisch, Fanatismus', in *Historisches Wörterbuch der Philosophie* 2, Basel and Stuttgart 1972, 904–7

Weitbrecht, H.J., *Psychiatrie im Grundriss*, Berlin [3]1973, 96

Global Fundamentalism: Sociological Perspectives

John Coleman

1. A sociological definition of fundamentalism

Global fundamentalism, expanding since the mid-1970s, took most sociologists by almost total surprise. It defied their earlier strong predictions about the course of modernity and modernization which forecast an ever increasing differentiation of strongly separate societal spheres (economy, polity, media, education, etc.) and the continuing growth of technical modes of rationality in almost all spheres of society. Global fundamentalism flew in the face of equally confident predictions about a growing world-wide trend toward secularization.

Unexpectedly, fundamentalism grew and continues to grow apace. In the United States (and, to a lesser extent, in Europe), evangelical fundamentalist churches grow faster than mainline Protestant and Catholic denominations.[1] In Latin America, fundamentalist Pentecostal churches have experienced four- and five-fold growth rates in the last thirty years. Since the 1960s, Latin America has been becoming Protestant more rapidly than Central Europe did in the sixteenth century.[2]

The rise of the Ayatollah Khomeini in Iran alerted sociologists to a virulent explosion of what, after 1979, came to be called 'Islamic fundamentalism'. In Israel, the growth and political power of *Gush Emumin* ('the bloc of the faithful') raises fears of a dangerous Jewish fundamentalism, especially after evidence was uncovered of attempts by adherents of *Gush Emumin* to blow up the mosque on the Dome of the Rock in Jerusalem. In India, Sikh and Hindu fundamentalists dispute the 'secular' nature of the Indian state as they engage in communal riots and selected acts of armed aggression.[3]

Even the geo-political changes wrought by the 1989 'velvet revolutions' in Eastern Europe have produced more, not less, promise for fundamentalisms. The new tribalisms now exposed in Eastern Europe show survivals of atavistic Russian Orthodox Tsarist rightist movements with core antisemitic beliefs. As the historian Martin Marty has noted, where these new tribalisms have religious roots, 'their religious dimensions are "fundamentalist" in impulse'.[4] In the post-Vatican II church, observers have also noted a revival of papal fundamentalism in groups such as Confrontatie in the Netherlands, Tradition, Family and Property in Latin America and Catholics United for the Faith in the United States. These new papal fundamentalist groups draw upon an earlier Catholic culture of integralism.[5]

Social scientists, in the last decade, have been assiduously studying these various fundamentalisms in comparative perspective. They seek to determine the organizational characteristics of fundamentalist movements (their various structures; size and social composition of members; recruitment processes; means of decision-making in the groups; modes of mobilizing resources and retaining the commitment of members). Sociologists also look to the changing world views, ideologies and programmes of the various fundamentalisms. Clearly, fundamentalism is of both religious and political import. Equally clearly, the global growth of fundamentalism in varying religious families, at the same time, cannot be totally by chance.

In most modern languages the term fundamentalism is *per se* pejorative: what we would call our opponents and not call ourselves. Fundamentalism evokes pejorative epithets such as reactionary, authoritarian, unreasonable, literalist, non-cosmopolitan, anti-modern, even paranoid, which can allow an easy dismissal of fundamentalism as an important modern and global phenomenon.

Despite serious objections to using the term in comparative perspective, it has gained a certain currency in comparative studies. Among many competing and – sometimes – purely stipulative definitions, I would propose the following definition and account of fundamentalism by the sociologists Anton Shupe and Jeffrey Hadden as a helpful basis for comparative studies of fundamentalisms.

> In simplest terms, we define fundamentalism as a proclamation of reclaimed authority over a sacred tradition which is to be reinstated as an antidote for a society that has strayed from its structural moorings. Sociologically speaking, fundamentalism involves: (1) a refutation of the radical differentiation of the sacred and the secular that has evolved with modernization and (2) a plan to dedifferentiate this institutional bi-furcation and thus bring religion back to center stage as an important factor or interest in public policy decisions.[6]

Fundamentalism involves a proclamation of reclaimed authority over a sacred tradition. It differs from utopian calls to create a new, heretofore totally imagined, social order. Fundamentalists call the people to return to a lost tradition. They call for the reclaiming of the values of a more pristine, allegedly more integral, earlier era. They seek thereby to reorient society and culture toward a more desirable future. The reconstructed earlier era may, of course, be highly idealized or depend on a very innovative over-emphasis on one or other trait of the imagined earlier era. Scientific historians may be hard put to discover the evidence for the alleged idealized past now selectively retrieved.

If in an earlier period there existed a more ideal and more moral society, fundamentalists must necessarily give an account of how the social order went astray. Fundamentalist ideologies or world-views, then, identify symbols of evil. They locate and condemn alternate ideologies, social movements and forces or individuals who have steered society away from the idealized past moral state. Concepts related to 'moral breakdown' and the corruption of values abound in fundamentalist discourse. At times, these are linked to alleged conspiracies of opponents labelled 'modernists' or 'secular humanists'.

Fundamentalists try to present continuities between their fundamenta-list movement and the faith tradition which it proclaims that it wants to restore. The core symbols evoked by the fundamentalist reactions are generally also central to the religion's orthodoxy. Thus, for example, *sola scriptura* become inerrant scripture or papal primacy become papal fundamentalism link the fundamentalisms to mainline Protestantism or Catholicism, where they have potential allies. To be sure, Catholic integralists and Protestant fundamentalists tend to stretch the orthodox symbols out of proportion and create a caricature of them. Still, fundamentalisms often feed back into the mainstream and are fed, in turn, by allies in the mainstream. Sometimes it is difficult to draw neat lines between fundamentalists and more nuanced traditionalists or conser-vatives. This ambiguity gives to fundamentalism a power beyond the radical fringe groups which espouse it wholly.

Importantly, fundamentalism is a modern phenomenon. In the process of undertaking a restoration in contemporary, demographic and technolo-gical conditions, new social orders are actually being promulgated.[7] Thus, for example, the Islamic Revolution of the Ayatollah Khomeini is not actually modelled on some ancient theocratic system which once existed in ancient Persia. It is not an embodiment of some mediaeval Islamic ideal. As Daniel Pipes has noted, 'Fundamentalists make Islam into something larger and more influential than anyone had previously understood.'[8] In particular, the idea of a single individual holding both supreme religious and executive power, as espoused by Khomeini, is an innovation in Islam.[9]

Similarly, American evangelical televangelists do not simply represent traditional evangelical Christianity on the television screens. Although they appeal to the 'old-time gospel', they weave new theologies and join political movements which represent a variety of social issues which reflect the twentieth century and an urban phenomenon: abortion, the Cold War, the growing power of the welfare state. As Shupe and Hadden put it, 'fundamentalism is a vigorous attempt to use aspects of a religious tradition for both coping with and reshaping the changing world'.[10]

Unlike world-rejecting sects and cults, fundamentalists seek to live in modernity (and influence its direction) but not be part of it. In a seminal essay comparing Catholic papal fundamentalism to Protestant evangelical fundamentalism, Daniel Alexander notes that fundamentalists reject a simple bipolar opposition between themselves and the modernists. They 'feel that there is not a bipolar opposition between good conservatives and modernist extremists, but rather a tripartite structure: on the right are those who turn their backs on their own era, whom they call traditionalists; on the extreme left are those who are ready to sacrifice everything to modernity, whom they call the modernists because they misunderstand their own era. In between the two, the fundamentalists claim to find the correct balance.'[11]

Thus, fundamentalists, typically, do not see themselves as simply reactionary. Rather, they refuse to acquiesce in the inevitability of change, a refusal which expresses a will to shape the world in a way that is different from modern forces. It is this active will to shape a different world that distinguishes fundamentalism from mere traditionalism.

Fundamentalism also has important differences from conservatism. Indeed, frequently it may be the genuine conservatives of the religious tradition who serve as the most powerful defence against fundamentalists, since they see the extent to which fundamentalists are really 'innovators' and not mere conservatives. A conservative Catholic, for example, misses in papal fundamentalism the older Catholic notion of a hierarchy of truths and different theological notes to authoritative pronouncements. Conservative Baptists in the Southern Baptist denomination in the United States resist the innovating political stands of the fundamentalists in their denomination who reject the traditional Baptist notion of a separation of church and state.[12]

2. Fundamentalism and modernity

Fundamentalism, as opposed to traditionalism, is a modern phenomenon. As the sociologist Nancy Ammerman has put it, 'Fundamentalism only exists where there is a conscious opposition to forces of change and conscious opposition can only exist where there *are* forces of change.'[13] Fundamentalists who seek to recreate inside the religious world what is no longer viable in the world outside, typically, maintain an ambiguous attitude towards modernity.

They reject a world view of modernity which equates it, without remainder, with 'rationality, pluralism, cosmopolitanism, progressivism and secularism'.[14] Like modernizing traditional elites in Third World societies, however, fundamentalists often desire full access to the technical tools of modernity while rejecting modernity's values. This, after all, was the stance of the Meiji restoration in nineteenth-century Japan. In this aspect, fundamentalists are quite similar to modernizing traditional elites in other settings.

Protestant fundamentalists in the United States have developed a highly sophisticated electronic church. They raise funds through state-of-the-art direct targeting market techniques. They take the modern business corporation as a model for church organization and expansion. They utilize the most modern organizational techniques to make their case in the political arena. Fundamentalists in our modern world use the most up-to-date techniques for resource mobilization of funds, recruits and the dissemination of their religio-political message. Khomeini could not have happened without the tape recorder. Some Catholic papal funda-mentalists, e.g. *Opus Dei*, are often members of technocratic elites.

Fundamentalists use the tools of modernity to negotiate with it – to cope with it, keep it at bay, turn back selected elements of its secularized differentiated world-view which keeps religion aloof from economics, politics and international affairs. Indeed, the active will of fundamentalists to shape a different world and not merely acquiesce in modernity is, already, a highly modern notion.

Some sociologists have argued that fundamentalists, far from imped-ing modernity, actually sometimes accelerate its course. Fundamental-ism, to be sure, is a way station between traditionalism as such and modernity. Thus, for example. David Martin sees Protestant fundamentalists in Latin America as seed carriers of a structural differ-entiation between religion and the polity which will relegate religion to cultural and individual spheres but differentiate the polity from the kind of direct religious influence typical of traditional Catholic societies. Martin sees the proliferating fundamentalist Protestant groups in Guatemala and elsewhere as germ cells for a new Protestant ethic imbued with the cultural logic of participation, voluntarism, self-government, personal initiative and capitalism so characteristic of modernity.[15] Clearly, we should not be so misled by the anti-modern restorationist motifs in fundamentalist discourse as to become blinded to

the multiple ways fundamentalism is a modern phenomenon and frequently propagates elements of modernity as it resists others.

3. Fundamentalism and secularization

The growth of global fundamentalism puts serious question marks around
claims that modernity necessarily entails an increased secularization. As
Rodney Stark and William Bainbridge argue, 'secularization, even in a
scientific age, . . .is a self-limitation process'.[16] Stark and Bainbridge's
point is that economic and political forces of so-called modernization and
secularization contain the germ of a reaction which brings religion back to
central concerns. The secular, the differentiated without new integration,
is itself the cause of a resacralization process. Often, although not
exclusively, fundamentalist groups stand at the forefront of this resacralization process.

To be sure, the secularization theory in sociology is more of a hodge-
podge of loosely employed ideas than a systematically tested theory. It
postulates that some things about modernity (e.g. urbanization, in-
dustrialization, differentiation) inevitably bring about the decline of
religion. Resurgent fundamentalism, among other phenomena, throws
cold water on this theory.

Some powerful evidence exists to suggest that new recruits to
fundamentalist movements (like converts to new religions more generally)
are the young, recent arrivals to communities without deep community ties
and those outside major power centres of decision-making in modern
society.[17] One study of evangelical fundamentalists in North America
shows that rejection of modernity thrives most among newcomers to urban
centres where 'exposure to diversity and change is high and resources to
deal with this newfound diversity and change are low'.[18] Clearly,
fundamentalists contest the inevitability of secularization in modern
conditions. They seek to infuse new energy into sacred traditions
perceived as under assault.

Karl Dobblelaere, the Louvain sociologist, connects secularization to
functional differentiation in modern society. 'The higher the degree of
functional differentiation in a society, the more advanced secularization
will be and the less impact religious organizations will be able to exert on
the culture.'[19]

Fundamentalists contest the differentiation process. In a paradox,
however, the more they try to oppose differentiation with effective modern
means, the greater the danger of a superficial accommodation with
elements of modernity. As a world-transforming movement, fundamentalism seeks effectively to transform the world. Over time, it is likely to be

subject to an irony of religion: every religion which tries to transform the world will be itself transformed in the process by the world. There is strong evidence, for example, that socially mobile American fundamentalists (in general, as a statistical group, the entire evangelical-fundamentalist population in America is undergoing social mobility) have, as the result of their higher education, become more liberal in attitudes towards sex, gender relations and race than their older co-religionists or those more marginal from a status position which can effect society.[20]

4. Global fundamentalism and globalization

In a number of important research articles, the sociologist Roland Robertson links the global rise of fundamentalism to the process of globalization itself. Globalization theory postulates the increasing con-solidation of nations and societies into an integrated evolving *world-system* of economic, political, technical inter-dependence. The world is becom-ing, in the cliché phrase, a global village.

Robertson draws upon globalization theory to describe a series of processes by 'which the world becomes a single place, both with respect to recognition of a very high degree of interdependence between spheres and locales of social activity across the entire globe and the growth of consciousness pertaining to the globe as such'.[21] Globalization, in a world-systems theory, presupposes secularization.

But, as Robertson sees it, 'There is an emerging problem of the definition of the global human situation. The increasing sense of shared fate in the modern world rests, primarily, upon material aspects of rapidly increasing global interdependence and conflicts associated with the distribution of material and political power. On the other hand, notwith-standing recent developments relevant to the embryonic crystallization across national boundaries of modes of discourse concerning, in the broadest sense, the meaning of the modern global human circumstance, global consciousness is indeed relatively unformed in comparison with the mere sense impression of material interdependence.'[22] Globalization demands a new sense of meaning, including religious meaning. Purely secular or materialist accounts do not suffice.

In a co-authored article, Robertson sums up the paradox of globaliza-tion. 'The modern state "invites" religious encroachment, precisely but not wholly because it is increasingly concerned with matters traditionally associated with the religious domain. Strict differentiation is not working! Moreover, the globalization process itself raises religious and quasi-religious questions.'[23] The regnant secular paradigms for modern polities and economies do not allow these questions to be systematically and seriously entertained!

Fundamentalism addresses classic issues of group boundaries and identity in a world undergoing a clear process of globalization but which lacks any deeper meaning than an imputed material interdependence. Robertson comments to this point:

> With respect to both the exacerbation of concern with societal identities (synchronically in relation to other societies and diachronically in relation to the historical 'mission' of the particular society) and the nature of individual attachment to one's own society, it would be expected that societies in the modern world would experience fundamentalist movements which make special claims to exhibit the 'real' identity of society in question and also, perhaps, the 'true' meaning to be given to the global circumstance. Indeed, we have witnessed the proliferation of such movements across the globe in recent years – some of them being explicitly concerned not merely with the identity of the societies in which they have arisen but also with the positive and negative identities of *other* societies in the international system – indeed, with the meaning of the global condition itself. My argument is that the fundamentalist and absolutist religious (and non-religious) movements of our time should be seen in terms of global developments and not simply in terms of their being reactions to particular *Gesellschaft* trends which a large number of societies have in common.[24]

Robertson, here, is appealing to a variant of 'strain theory' in sociology which explains the expansion of ideologically strong social movements by assuming that they serve as a lens to mirror real strains in social integration. In this case, the strain is the lack of a new integrative meaning system for the new global economic and political interdependence. Absent alternative voices in providing meaning for this new dislocation of received world-views and discourses, fundamentalism enters the arena with its own preferred meaning system.

The fundamental social significance of global fundamentalism, then, may lie less in trying to understand fearful and authoritarian responses to strange and new social and cultural phenomena. Dismissing fundamentalism by such essentially reductionistic psychological categories is a major mistake. The challenge is to see how fundamentalists have entered an important vacuum of meaning about globalization as a process and about the particular identities of peoples and nations and societies as this new inter-dependence grows, devoid of any deeper meaning system.

The challenge is, certainly, also to more mainstream religion to address the same issues – perhaps with utopias as well as restorationist world-views

– and certainly with more nuance. No less than fundamentalists can other adherents of religion accept as meaningful a differentiation which allows no further integration. No less can they accept modernity as a holistic and ideological framework since it is, as that, bankrupt. An astute and sympathetic student of Islamic fundamentalist movements has put it this way for us: 'Though its adherents are unlikely to prevail, their brief moments of public notoriety will cause others to re-think the quandaries posed by the technical age, and in the High Tech Era we may yet dare to hope for the emergence of a universalist vision that admits the authenticity of the motives of the fundamentalists [to achieve some new integration beyond secularization and differentiation through technical rationality] without surrendering to their apocalyptic conclusions.'[25] In the crunch, I am not so sure I prefer Max Weber's image of an iron cage of modernity to the fundamentalist hope to address a new integration beyond all the differentiations. If the proferred integration may be a bit simplistic or idealized, it nevertheless addresses real issues in our modern world. Would that the mainline churches were addressing them as seriously!

Notes

1. Dean Kelley, *Why the Conservative Churches are Growing*, New York 1972.
2. David Stoll, *Is Latin America Turning Protestant?* Berkeley, Ca. 1990.
3. For *Gush Emunim*, cf. Ian Lustick, *The Land and the Lord: Jewish Fundamentalism in Israel*, New York 1988; for Islamic fundamentalism see James Piscatori (ed.), *Islam in the Political Process*, New York 1983.
4. Martin Marty, 'The Fundamentalism Project at Midpoint', *Criterion*, Winter 1990, 21.
5. For papal fundamentalism see Peter Hebblethwaite, 'A Roman Catholic Fundamentalism', *The Times Literary Supplement*, 4 August 1988, and my 'Who are the Catholic Fundamentalists?', *Commonweal*, 27 January 1989, 42–7.
6. Anton Shupe and Jeffrey Hadden (eds.), *Secularization and Fundamentalism Reconsidered*, Vol. III, New York 1989, 111.
7. *Ibid.*, 112ff.
8. Daniel Pipes, 'Fundamentalist Moslims in World Politics', in *Secularization and Fundamentalism Reconsidered*, Vol. III, 124.
9. Piscatori, *Islam* (n. 3), 215, makes this claim for the innovation of Khomeini.
10. Shupe and Hadden, *Secularization* (n. 6), 113.
11. Daniel Alexander, 'Is Fundamentalism an Integralism?', *Social Compass*, Winter 1985.
12. Nancy Ammerman, *Baptist Battles*, New Brunswick, NJ 1990.
13. *Ibid.*, 155.
14. For this characterization of modernity see Martin Marty, *Modern American Religion: The Irony of it All*, Chicago 1986.
15. David Martin, *Tongues of Fire: The Explosion of Protestantism in Latin America*, Oxford 1990.

16. Rodney Stark and William Bainbridge, *The Future of Religion*, Berkeley, Ca. 1985, 2.

17. Nancy Ammerman, *Bible Believers: Fundamentalist Believers in the Modern World* New Brunswick, NJ 1987.

18. Ammerman, *Baptist Battles* (n. 12), 167.

19. Karl Dobblelaere, 'The Secularization of Society? Some Methodological Suggestions', in *Secularization and Fundamentalism Reconsidered*, Vol. III, 29.

20. For the effect of education in making American fundamentalists more liberal in religion see James D. Hunter, *Evangelicalism: The Coming Generation*, New York 1986.

21. Roland Robertson, 'The Sacred and the World System', in Phillip Hammond, (ed.) *The Sacred in a Secular Age*, Berkeley, Ca. 1985.

22. Roland Robertson, 'A New Perspective on Religion and Secularization in the Global Context', in *Secularization and Fundamentalism Reconsidered*, Vol. III, 69.

23. Roland Robertson and JoAnn Chirico, 'Human Globalization and the World-Wide Religious Resurgence: A Theoretical Explanation', in *Sociological Analysis* 46, Fall 1985, 225 and 239.

24. Robertson, 'A New Perspective on Religion and Secularization in the Global Context' (n. 22), 65.

25. Bruce Lawrence, *Defenders of God: The Fundamentalist Revolt Against the Modern Age*, New York 1989, 244.

II · Jewish Fundamentalism

What is the Challenge of Contemporary Jewish Fundamentalism?

Jacob Neusner

1. A questionable term

A Protestant Christian theological category, 'fundamentalism' bears no point of obvious relevance to any contemporary Judaisms. To no Judaism today, whether Reform, Reconstructionist, Conservative, Orthodox in any of the numerous Orthodox Judaisms now flourishing, is the proposition of the literal, inerrant veracity of scripture, read in its own terms and framework, an option. The reason is that all Judaisms approach the Hebrew Scriptures, known in Judaisms as the written Torah, through the way set forth by the oral Torah, now preserved in written form in the two Talmuds and various Midrash-compilations; and in the reading of the oral Torah, while the written Torah is always true, it is never read in a literal manner, such as the Protestant fundamentalist hermeneutic maintains it should be. Consequently, in a narrow sense, we cannot speak of fundamentalism in the context of any Judaism, or, therefore, of Judaism in general.

But so far as fundamentalism refers to a broader phenomenon than the hermeneutical one suggests, we may identify points of congruence in recent developments among Judaisms and counterparts in various Christianities and Islams. For among Judaisms in our day, issues have been raised in a vivid way that, in general, people supposed were no longer subject to debate. And we find that questions thought closed very vividly precipitate violent argument. So far as we may identify as 'fundamentalism' a renewal of debate on the basic questions of social organization of the faith, the Judaic social order, we may say that there is a fundamentalism that flourishes among contemporary Judaisms, and it is a considerable challenge to the Judaic social order, on the one side, and to the position of the Judaic religious composite among other religious composites, on the other.

2. Integration or segregation?

Specifically, from the end of the eighteenth century, most Jews in Western Europe, the USA, the Western hemisphere, north and south, as well as in the outlying communities in South Africa, Australia, New Zealand, and elsewhere, took for granted that they wished to be both Judaic and something more, indeed, many things more. The received social theory of Judaism, that Jews were always Judaic and also *only* Judaic, had yielded a social order in which Israel, the holy people, dwelt alone, that is, segregated. From the nineteenth century forward, a variety of Judaisms took shape that set forth an integrationist account: Jews were to be both Judaic and a variety of other things: citizens, for instance, of their native countries; participants in the cultural life of those countries; fully integrated in most ways into the cultural and social life of those countries. The earliest debates within the Zionist mode of Judaism, too, took for granted that the Jewish state would form a political entity on its own, but would also take its place within the larger framework of cosmopolitan culture; German was considered as the language of the state, for instance, and Kenya its location.

The essentially segregationist conception of the Judaic social order put forth by the canonical writings of Judaism, that is, the oral and written Torah read whole, persisted, of course, and indeed predominated so long as it was politically feasible in such countries as Poland, Russia, Roumania and Austria-Hungary, where most Jews lived. With the advent of Communism in the Soviet Union, on the one hand, and the annihilation, between 1939 and 1945, of most of European Jewry by the Germans and their local allies, the vast, mostly segregated Judaic world of those countries perished. Communism would not tolerate Judaism, nor Nazism Jews. So, after 1945, people generally assumed that all Judaisms would take the integrationist view. Orthodox Judaisms in the West, and in the state of Israel, made their peace with integration, with the paramount form of Orthodox Judaism taking its place, in politics, among the Zionist political parties of the state of Israel.

In the past twenty years, however, it is clear that segregationist Judaisms have come to the fore, and in so far as these represent a reaffirmation of the fundamental social order envisaged by the Judaism of the dual Torah, these Judaisms do constitute a contemporary Judaic fundamentalism. They call into question the settlement that the vast majority of Jews living in Western lands have taken for granted: Jews would be different from other citizens of their countries in some, few ways, but integrated in all ways. That is, they would differ in religion, but religion would then affect only some few aspects of the common life, and these would be mostly personal, private and individual. On that basis, the Western countries found they could accommodate vast and diverse populations, including populations with a variety of religions, among them Judaism.

3. Characteristics of segregationist Judaisms

In the USA in some numbers, in the state of Israel in large numbers, and in some European countries in negligible numbers, communities flourish today which are formed around segregationist Judaisms. They do not constitute a single social entity, one Judaism: some of these Judaisms are Zionist, most not; some are Hassidic, many not. Some form large communities, others small. So to identify them as a single Judaism, among Judaisms, errs as much as assuming that all Judaisms form one Judaism. But among the variety of segregationist Judaisms a few traits prove characteristic.

1. *All reject all forms of intercourse with the world beyond*. In the case of some segregationist Judaisms in the USA, adherents work in some few, scheduled occupations, travelling to work together in buses; live in buildings and neighbourhoods in which they alone predominate; patronize only their own stores; turn only to their own professional services (e.g., in medicine and the like). In the case of Israeli counterparts, entire villages and even towns are comprised of only segregationists.

2. All take an *exclusive view of truth*, seeing Judaism as the only valid statement by God to humanity and, among Judaisms, of course, only their own.

3. *All reject the conception of politics as an exercise in the pursuit of goals shared among various persons*, seeing the political world as an opportunity for the improvement of the condition of their own situation, on the one side, or as source of a threat to the community's autonomy and integrity, on the other. In the USA the former attitude prevails, and the segregationist Judaisms participate actively in the political life of city, state, and nation, in common with many other identifiable groups forming a political subset in American politics but, unlike all other Jews, setting themselves apart from the rest of the Jewish community. In the state of Israel, the latter attitude has produced the formation of non-Zionist and even anti-Zionist political parties. In both cases, segregationist theology produces a politics of remarkably limited perspective.

The challenge of segregationist Judaisms faces both the world of Judaisms on the one side and the social order of the USA and the State of

Israel on the other. Integrationist Judaisms find it possible to collaborate on shared tasks of common interest. Segregationist Judaisms do not. Integrationist Judaisms express Jews' broadly held aspirations to participate in the common life of their countries. Moreover they sustain, in the framework of Jewry, the generally-held attitude of Western democracies that all citizens share a common interest and bear fealty to the common good; above and beyond difference, whether of race or religion, a single definition of what society requires prevails. That theory of the social order now faces the challenge of Judaisms that recognize no such commonality with all Jews or with gentiles. None can doubt that other ways of conducting the public business besides the one presently paramount may serve. But the theory of the relationships between and among diverse religious groups, and within a given religious framework (the Judaic, the Christian, the Muslim), vastly differs from the one that has sustained democracy as we have known it.

The challenge of segregationist Judaisms in the state of Israel to the political integrity of the state, like that addressed by those Judaisms to the conception of a single cogent Jewish community – and community of Judaism – in the USA and Western Europe, raises fundamental issues of a theological character: what we mean by 'Israel', the holy people, how we recognize God's image and likeness in the other (the one who is different, whether Jew or gentile), and what we are to do together in this life, in this time, in this place. These prove challenges of not so much an intellectual as a social and political character, and the consensus of ideas and attitudes that have sustained the social order as we know it in the West today, whether in the state of Israel or in Western Europe or in the USA, no longer prevails. What is to come none can now say, but, it is clear that we are entering interesting times.

What shall be the Answer to Contemporary Jewish Fundamentalism?

Samuel E. Karff

Incontestably, the overwhelming majority of Jews in the world reject the fundamentalist perspective Jacob Neusner has so clearly defined. Most eschew a segregationist mode of existence and seek to share fully the burdens and privileges of civic life. Most seek respectful accommodation with other Jews and gentiles. Most gladly include themselves in the social contract which binds diverse groups in a pluralistic society and accept some responsibility for the commonweal. How then shall we respond to a fundamentalist rejectionism which casts doubt on our Jewish legitimacy?

1. Reaffirm the pluralistic traditions in Judaism

Such rejectionism is reflected in attempts to force a change in Israel's 'Law of Return' and deny those converted to Judaism by 'inauthentic' rabbis the privilege of automatic Israeli citizenship. Other less widely publicized attempts at 'delegitimatizing' include a rabbinic ruling that professors from a non-Orthodox Jewish seminary must not be permitted to lecture at an Orthodox synagogue lest heretical teachings be imparted, and a ruling that one who attends a non-Orthodox synagogue on Rosh Hashanah has not fulfilled the obligation to hear the shofar (ram's horn) properly sounded. Similar examples could be multiplied.

The most constructive initial response to such rejectionism is to reaffirm to ourselves from within the tradition itself the peril and perniciousness of the fundamentalist temper. The Talmud admonishes that the Temple in Jerusalem was destroyed by 'groundless hatred' of Jew for fellow Jew. Elsewhere the destruction is attributed to judgments of Jewish law that lacked compassion and breadth.

There is also some warrant within classic Jewish texts for the respectful accommodation of diverse perspectives. A much cited Mishnah attests that the school of Shammi and the school of Hillel disagreed on many matters, including marital eligibility. One school permitted what the others prohibited and declared eligible whom the others deemed ineligible. Nevertheless, 'the men of Shammi did not refrain from marrying women from families of the school of Hillel, nor did the men of Hillel refrain from marrying the women of Shammi'.

Such pluralistic motifs within classic texts are especially welcome when cited by scholars who define themselves as Orthodox (but not fundamentalist). Eliezer Berkovits and David Hartman are notably in this category. While such argumentation will not persuade the fundamentalist, it is an important antidote to self-doubt and demoralization within the non-fundamentalist Jewish camp.

2. Constructive self-criticism

But steadfastly and cogently arguing against fundamentalist attempts at delegitimatizing the rest of us is not sufficient. We non-fundamentalist Jews must also address troubling issues within our own camp and not flinch from constructive self-criticism. This is especially the case for those who define ourselves as non-Orthodox (or liberal) Jews. An argument advanced by the fundamentalists is that their restrictive interpretation of covenantal norms is alone legitimate and is the only way of preserving Judaism and the Jewish people from corrosive assimilation in a non-Jewish world.

To counter that claim by asserting that Jewish survival over the centuries was in fact enhanced by creative, sometimes radical reinterpretation of covenant norms is valid but also not sufficient. We must grant that if excessive rigidity is an enemy of Jewish vitality and survival, so is a flabby accommodationism which knows no boundaries and has lost the power to say 'no' to the larger culture or to ourselves.

Let the fundamentalist attack engender a soul-searching quest for a more responsible liberal posture which grounds its deviations from halachic (Jewish legal) norms in classic Jewish texts, seeks to validate a selective embrace of contemporary cultural norms (women's empowerment – including women rabbis) by appealing to basic Jewish values (the dignity of man and woman under God) and which demonstrates that Jewish liberalism not only builds bridges to the larger culture but has the muscle to define boundaries.

3. Promote Jewish inclusivism

Clearly, however, the answer to Jewish fundamentalism may not be limited to either a reaffirmation of our authenticity or constructive self-criticism.

The Jewish community has in place institutional structures designed to promote a Jewish inclusivism that transcends our denominational divisions and counters the exclusivist posture of Jewish fundamentalists. These structures are based on the premise that Jews share a common fate even when we disagree on issues of *halacha* and belief. In our time Hitler made no distinction between fundamentalist and non-fundamentalist Jews, Orthodox and non-Orthodox, believers and professed atheists.

Living in a post-Holocaust world has made pragmatic Zionists of the overwhelming majority of world Jewry. Sentiment is divided on the most viable way to accommodate the just claim of Palestinian Arabs, but commitment to Israel's survival and well-being, and enabling all Jews in need of refuge to resettle there, is an agenda around which world Jewry has rallied.

In most Jewish communities in the West there is a communal federation that brings together Orthodox, Conservative and Reform Jews as well as the non-synagogued. The funds raised by such federations support projects in Israel and the local community. A substantial portion of those funds are allocated to local Jewish educational institutions. A complete study has yet to be made of the impact of such federations in uniting an ideologically disparate Jewish community and maintaining a pragmatic pluralism within its ranks. Some fundamentalist Jewish institutions have sought and received funding for their schools. They feel dependent upon the resources of the non-fundamentalist Jewish community and therefore must prudently refrain from strident attacks on alternate Judaisms. In effect this arrangement has moderated public attack and preserved a high level of civility, especially within the American diaspora.

The leverage of the Council of Jewish Federations and Welfare Funds (an amalgam of local federations) was clearly felt in the most recent attempt some years ago to exclude non-Orthodox Jewish converts from the 'Law of Return'. The fundamentalists in Israel and the United States sparked the battle. In response, mainstream Orthodox groups united with non-Orthodox Jewish organizations to prevent an outcome that could have alienated a majority of American Jews from Israel. The Council of Jewish Federations articulated a strong position in favour of inclusiveness and, on this issue, the Israeli government did not surrender to the fundamentalists' demands.

Generally, Jewish fundamentalists cannot prevail in the consensus-oriented pluralistic structures of the American Jewish community, nor can they exert a coercive influence here. Unfortunately, the vagaries of the electoral system do grant them disproportionate weight in Israel today. However, since most Israelis do not share the fundamentalist agenda, there is hope that, over time, this anomalous situation will not prevail.

Potentially, one of the most significant challenges to the fundamentalists' agenda could come from a religiously based Jewish umbrella organization composed of Reform, Conservative and mainstream Orthodox Jews. Officially the Synagogue Council of America (SCA) is such an instrumentality.

Since each of the constitutent groups maintains a veto power, the SCA must function by total consensus. The organization has been most visible in asserting a common religious concern for the security of Israel and has represented the Jewish community in consultations with ecumenical Protestant groups and with the Catholic Church. Periodically the Orthodox groups within SCA have felt pressed from the right to abandon this structure. Thus far such pressures have been resisted. It may safely be said that the overwhelming majority of American Jews endorse the existence of such an ecumenical Jewish organization. Delicately balanced and limited though it is, the SCA represents an important Jewish response to the self-segregating philosophy of Jewish fundamentalists.

4. Jews and gentiles

Since fundamentalists not only seek to segregate themselves from fellow Jews but accept only the most limited pragmatic-instrumental engagement with the gentile world, a response is required in this sphere as well. To be sure, most Jews have voted with their feet. The Jewish community, especially in the West, has adopted the integrationist mode residentially, vocationally and politically. Most Jews seek a balance between turning inward to synagogue and Jewish educational and social institutions for a nourishing covenantal particularism and reaching out to share in the larger inter-religious and socio-political community.

Many rabbis participate in inter-religious clergy associations and some in dialogue groups. Church groups are invited to congregational Passover Seders, and in the United States there are many inter-faith Thanksgiving Day services. Those occasions pose an interesting challenge in themselves: how to develop a liturgy that will neither offend the other nor diminish one's distinctive religious witness.

An earlier liturgical consensus for such inter-religious services was grounded on the asymmetrical relation between Judaism and Christianity: Christians could pray to the God of Israel, but inter-faith prayer must avoid christological language. That consensus has been increasingly questioned by Christian clergy, who feel that it violates the integrity of their faith. The American inter-religious scene is further challenged and enriched by a growing Islamic and Buddhist presence. In any case, where inter-religious worship and dialogue is possible,

Jewish participation constitutes a constructive symbolic answer to Jewish fundamentalism.

Even more symbolically significant than what we pray when we are together is the way we allude to each other in our respective liturgies. Christian liturgies which preserve vestiges of the New Testament Jewish-Christian polemic have been alienating and offensive to Jews. To its credit, through liturgical reform the Christian church has evidenced sensitivity in this area. Comparable sensitivity has been most evident in non-Orthodox Jewish liturgy. Here again the non-fundamentalist Jew should draw on evidence within the tradition itself that God's truth is imparted not only to the Jewish people. The Talmudic benediction which thanks God for the wisdom revealed to a gentile sage is embodied in the following prayer from the Reform liturgy: 'We give thanks for the sages and teachers of all peoples and faiths who have brought many to a deeper understanding of You and Your will.'

5. Shared responsibility for justice and peace

Finally, there is that Jewish response to fundamentalism grounded in our shared responsibility for justice and peace in the social order. Such inter-religious social action reached its peak in the United States during the civil rights era in the 1960s, when conferences on religion and race lent the weight of God's word to the quest for racial justice. To this day there remains much consultation and co-operation by United States church and synagogue groups in promoting a shared vision of the social order. The efforts are, of course, complicated by issues that divide us (church-state, Israel, etc.). Nevertheless, non-fundamentalist Jews do answer the challenge of contemporary Jewish fundamentalism when we manifest an active concern for the dignity and well-being of all God's children in the social order.

While the challenge of Jewish fundamentalism is certainly an area of concern, its ideology is not likely to prevail, certainly not in the United States and not even in Israel, unless the social order reverts to an ugly posture and the fundamentalist vision of an isolated Jewry in a hostile world attains grim plausibility. Barring that tragic scenario, the Jewish community is not likely to permit the fundamentalists to shape its destiny.

III · Islamic Fundamentalism

What is the Challenge of Contemporary Islamic Fundamentalism?

Elsayed Elshahed

This is an old and at the same time highly topical theme, which has been of great interest in recent years in the media as well as among scholars. Objectivity and unprejudiced analysis are requisites in discussing it.

In my view the term 'challenge' contained in the title needs some explanation, since it has aggressive overtones and in this context suggests a declaration of war on other religions by Islam, Islam claiming to have the leading position among the religions. History, at least, has shown that this claim, which any religion makes, may be realized in Islam exclusively with peaceful means. In the Qur'an we read: 'Call men to the part of your Lord with wisdom (*al-ḥikma*) and kindly exhortation (*al-mawʿiẓa al-ḥasana*). Reason with them in the most courteous manner' (surah 16/125). Muslims must be particularly careful in dealing with Jews and Christians: surah 29/46 reads: 'Be courteous when you argue with the people of the Book (*ahl al-kitāb*).' These two verses of the Qur'an are clearly an invitation to dialogue with those of other faiths, especially with Jews and Christians, and they determine the mode of procedure, which excludes any form of compulsion: 'There shall be no compulsion in religion. True guidance is now distinct from error' (2/256).

Accordingly the Qur'an expresses a readiness for peace and for dialogue with non-Muslims.

1. 'Fundamentalism' – a problematical term

When the term 'fundamentalism' is used today, it is generally used in a pejorative sense. When it is applied to the Muslim world, the West means by it the backward, the conservatives, the radicals.

This does not correspond to its originally philological significance (holding firm to the fundamentals).

For Muslims 'fundamentalism' is a particular discipline in Islamic science: it describes the discipline of jurisprudence (the method of arriving at a judgment, Arabic *uṣūl al fiqh*).

The 'fundamentalists' (*uṣūliyūn*) certainly persist in their own Islamic identity, but they can be quite progressive and open to other religions and cultures. However, this very persistence in their own identity is often negatively termed 'fundamentalist' by the West.

Conversely, on the Muslim side, the term 'fundamentalism' applied to the West is by no means clear. Many Muslims associate 'fundamentalism' with the absolute rule of the church and the misuse of religion from the fourth century to the Enlightenment.

In the West it is a mistake to condemn too rapidly any renewal movement or, as we call it, 're-Islamicization' or 'Islamism', as a fundamentalist movement in the narrow sense, and to attribute conservatism or radicalism to it. Muslim fundamentalism is not a 'popular movement of so-called simple people' but an area of Islamic religious study.

There are similarities between Muslim and Christian fundamentalists to the degree that like their Christian opposite numbers Muslims reject everything which puts in question the inerrancy of Holy Scripture.

However, in the Islamic view Muslim fundamentalism has the following advantages over Christian fundamentalism:

(*a*) Islam never fights against science. Scientists are never persecuted because of their findings; on the contrary, Islam makes the acquisition of any useful science the religious duty of every person capable of it. The prophet Muhammad puts the scientists second after the prophets: 'The scientists are the successors (or legitimate heirs) of the prophets' (*al-'ulamā'u waraṯatu l-anbiyā'*).

(*b*) In the Islamic view, science confirms the statements of the Qur'an, especially in the sphere of natural science. Therefore Muslims have no anxiety about science.

(*c*) If Muslims defend their holy scripture, the Qur'an, they do so because for them the Qur'an is an unfalsified, pure, divine revelation which is exalted above all errors. That opposition in Islamic countries is always understood by the governments in question and the West in the negative sense as a rebellion of Islamic fundamentalists and is described in these terms nourishes the conviction in the Islamic opposition that the West and the undemocratic regimes have common aims. This is one of the reasons for the fundamental mistrust by Muslims of the West and everything that comes out of the West.

Now when one talks of 'fundamentalism' in Islam, in addition it is necessary to differentiate between two trends:

(*a*) *salafiyah* (from *salaf* = the predecessors): this denotes a trend in Islam in which the contemporaries of the prophets and the later generation have a special exemplary status in Islam.

(*b*) *uṣuliyūn* (from *uṣūl* = foundations): this denotes the trend which refers to the primal sources of Islam (Qur'an and Sunna, the tradition of the Prophet).

To this degree I understand fundamentalism as a return to reflection on original Islam or, as the great Islamic renewal figure Abu Hamid al Gazzali (505/1111 CE) saw it, as a revival of religion.

In what follows I shall describe 'fundamentalism' understood in this way as Islamism, in order to avoid the misunderstandings to which the term fundamentalism leads.

2. In what does the challenge of Islamism consist?

1. Its teaching is simple and everyone can understand it. It is rational and free from complicated theories like the doctrines of the Trinity or original sin.

2. Its unambiguous confession of monotheism, belief in the only God, who is one in himself, who neither begets nor is begotten (see surah 112).

3. Belief in the message of all the prophets of revelation like Abraham, Moses, Jesus and finally Muhammad, whose key statements are contained in the Qur'an and have remained unfalsified up to the present day. That is the basis for its universal claim.

4. Its commandments and prohibitions have a rational foundation. A small part of them are regarded as an indication of total human submission to the divine will. These include the commands to fast for Ramadan and for some rites on pilgrimages.

5. Islam addresses all human needs in an appropriate way and offers a complete view of life in which faith and action are inseparable. The Qur'an states: 'Believers, why do you profess what you never do? It is most odious in God's sight that you should say one thing and do another' (61/3).

6. Islam not only offers man instructions but tells him how he should carry them out. This is particularly clear in the social or political sphere. Any legal action is at the same time a commandment which will be rewarded in this world and the world to come. So in the Qur'an one very often finds faith bound up with action. Surah 103/2–3 states: ' . . . perdition shall be the lot of man, except for those who have faith (in God) and do good works'.

7. In Islam man is responsible for his actions. If he sins he can always

ask God for forgiveness. God always forgives as long as man truly repents of his sin. 'God will not forgive those who serve other gods besides Him; but He will forgive whom He will for other sins' (4/48). 'Do not despair of God's mercy, for He forgives all sins' (39/53). 'He has decreed mercy for Himself' (6/12).

8. Islam offers a social system in which private and public life are integrated; i.e. it contains a political, economic and social system which are contained in a 'constitution', namely the Qur'an, in a simple codification. According to the Islamic view of the world, public and private life cannot be separated and thus secularized. As a prophet, the prophet Muhammad himself was a statesman, and in Medina he founded the first Islamic state with all the necessary organs.

9. Western civilization could not cope with the great problems at present facing humanity. Muslims see salvation only in the religion which satisfies all human needs, not only spiritual but also pastoral and material, in harmony and balance. Islam offers itself as a meaningful alternative.

10. Islam shows its capacity for adaptation to social changes conditioned by space and time through its varied methods of jurisprudence. The human spirit has great scope for solving problems.

Alongside the Qur'an and the Sunna, which are open to interpretation, there are other ways of solving problems if the Qur'an and the Sunna are not enough: *ijmāʿ*, consensus, *giās*, conclusions by analogy, and *ijtihād*, mental effort or reflection. The right of application is allowed to anyone capable of it and is not the privilege of a particular stratum or generation.

11. In the Islamic view, human freedom even from the claims of governments to domination is exclusively guaranteed by submission to the divine will. When the second caliph Omar entered office (12/634 CE), he said to those present in a mosque: 'I was chosen ruler over you. However, that does not mean that I am the best among you. Help me, as long as I rule over you by the instructions of the Qur'an and the Prophet, but if you detect any deviations in me, then put me back on the right way.' Then a non-Arab Muslim said: 'By God, if I noted any deviation in you, I would put you right again by my sword.'

Omar was also the first caliph to reject some Islamic punishments on humanitarian grounds, and made all the decisions that he could not derive from Qur'an or Sunna by taking counsel, *šūra*. These examples show that Islam recognizes neither dictatorship nor racism.

So as Hans Zirker rightly notes, in Islam the caliphs have 'neither a prophetic nor a magisterial function. Only Muslim society as a whole is to this degree said to have an infallible understanding of faith.'[1]

12. From an Islamic perspective the history of the development of Europe would have looked quite different if:

(*a*) The Gospels had contained definitive political, economic and social systems, or at least the beginnings of them.

(*b*) The church had not misused its power on scientists.

(*c*) Europe had taken over from Islam or Islamic culture not only its scientific and rational achievements but also the religious framework in which they were set.

Muslim Islamists ask themselves why Jews and Christians are touchy about anything Islamic and reject it *a priori*, although Islam recognizes the message at the heart of their religions as well as their prophets and treats these with full respect. Why do not Jews and Christians show Muslims the same respect? Why do they not acknowledge Islam at least as a supplement to their own religions of revelation?

3. Is re-Islamicization a mere reaction to the modern American and European world?

Re-Islamicization is usually understood as an emotional reaction to the American and European modern world-view, which has become excessively powerful. This understanding is correct only to the degree that the modern Western world overshadows all Islamic countries with the aid of its technical, political, military and economic superiority and threatens the Islamic consciousness. Nevertheless, history shows us that the situation within Islam is also encouraged by foreign influences and that these influences produce the decisive moment for any attempt at re-Islamicization. As Islam always has been and remains open to other cultures, Muslims must constantly take account of foreign influences and deviations. When these get beyond a certain level, Islam's own power of defence is automatically switched in and continues to function until the foreign influences and the deviations they have caused are restored to acceptable limits. The Prophet Muhammad foresaw these situations and said of them: 'God will send you one (or several at the same time) every hundred years, who will renew or revive your religion.' This is a prediction of the Prophet Muhammad which indicates the future internal weakness and negative influences and describes the process of renewal as something that belongs to Islam.

Through this process of renewal, in addition new possibilities of adapting the Islamic world-view to the social changes which have taken place in the meantime have been set in motion by the mental effort (*ijtihād*) of particular religious scholars. That is how the attempts at re-Islamicization by the 'fundamentalists' are to be understood. Without doubt the disappointment of Muslims at the consequences of Western civilization play a decisive role in the rise of 'fundamentalism'. The reasons for this disappointment can be summed up as follows:

1. Muslims feel that their religion is misunderstood by the West and that they are politically abused.

2. The opening of many Islamic countries towards the West has led to increasing political and economic dependence of these countries on the West. The poor are becoming increasingly poor and the rich richer. So there is an enormous social gulf and a high potential for conflict in these countries.

3. So-called development aid has been unmasked as self-help for the West. The recipients of this 'aid' get deeper into debt and accordingly become politically dependent.

4. Wherever Western modernity gets a footing, human beings lose their identity, culture, values and norms. Material values take the place of morality and social coherence.

5. Western support is mostly enjoyed only by despots, although the West claims to be encouraging democracy or democratization in these countries.

6. Western modernity has always been bound up with secularization. But this is generally rejected by Muslims. So modernization could not be regarded as progress, but would have to be seen as alienation or uprooting.

7. The one-sided partisan support for Israel by Western countries robs the West of any credibility among Muslims. Muslims understand the unjust Western support as open war against Islam, because for Muslims any political decision is a religious decision.

4. How should one deal with the Qur'an?

By Islamic conviction the Qur'an is the literal revelation of God fixed in writing in Arabic. It was revealed complete during the lifetime of the prophet Muhammad, learned off by heart by many of the prophets and fixed in writing. It is presented in many readings (*alsina*) but these do not affect the content in any way. It was collected and preserved immediately after the death of the prophet, until the third caliph Othman, with the help of Qur'an readers and scribes, was able to produce the text of the Qur'an which exists today.

There is no doubt about the authenticity of the Qur'an, at least as the proclamation of the prophet Muhammad. In the preface to his translation of the Qur'an Rudi Paret says that 'the text (of the Qur'an) is generally reliable and reproduces the wording which contemporaries heard from the mouth of the prophet'. For Islam and its whole legislation the Qur'an is, as Hans Küng says, 'something like the constitution, the fundamental law that cannot be read arbitrarily, even though it has given rise to a broad spectrum of interpretation by different people at different times in different places'.[2] 'The admonition to the prophets not to be over-hasty over the recitation of the received texts shows that the revelation was felt as a gift received by Muhammad positively, without any of his own involvement.'[3]

The verses of the Qur'an are sub-divided into two groups: 1. verses which contain religious duties (*'ibādāt*); 2. verses which order actions for this world (*mu'āmalāt*). In this way it offers a plan for this world and the beyond in a coherent, balanced form of life. Different types of interpretations of the Qur'an make it understandable to all Muslims. Muhammad himself was the first interpreter of the Qur'an. This prophetic interpretation is not only the first but at the same time the most reliable. It is contained in the tradition (*ḥadīṯ* = Sunna).

The verses of the Qur'an are again divided into two further types:

1. Straightforward and absolutely clear verses (*muḥkamāt*).

2. Verses which are capable of interpretation or in need of explanation (*muta ašābihāt*).

There is unanimity among Muslim interpreters and above all legal experts and educated Muslims on the first type of Qur'an verses. The second, however, are interpreted in different ways. Thus they allow the human understanding to apply its faculties.

The clear verses are mainly those which determine the distribution of the estate of a dead person, which lay down the times for prayers, fasts and pilgrimages, and the level of the tax for the poor, the rewards for good deeds or the punishments for evil deeds in this world and the world to come; the regulations for marriage and divorce; and, importantly, the regulations for contracts relating to buying, selling, debts on or investment of one's own possessions or those of another, especially orphans and the elderly, and peace treaties.

The proportion of these regulations in the verses of the Qur'an is very small compared with those which are capable of interpretation, and which determine the social life of a Muslim.

The Muslim insistence that the Qur'an is the literal revelation of God has protected the Qur'an from being falsified and relativized.

A convinced Muslim does not dissent from this principle of faith, since he knows that otherwise the Qur'an would suffer the relativizing that the other holy scriptures have undergone. In my view the demand for a new understanding of the Qur'an as not being a literal revelation, on the pretext of adapting it to modern life, is unfounded, because this adaptation already was and is possible through interpretations. So the text cannot be relativized and altered at will.

Islam has been dominant for many centuries in the various cultural groups and has shown its capacity to keep them at the highest level of contemporary civilization. This has happened without any interference with the original text of the Qur'an.

The well-known Imam as-Šafi'ī (204/824) already showed that the Islamic law can be adapted to changed social and contemporary circumstances by founding two different legal schools, one for Egypt and one for Iraq.

The abolition or at least the relativizing of Islamic penal law (al-ḥudūd aš-šarʿiya) could be the background to such a demand. However, for this there is no need either to alter or to relativize the text of the Qur'an. There is a basic principle for all Islamic rulings to the effect that in emergencies even what is prohibited can be regarded as permissible and vice versa (aḍ-ḍarūrāt tubīḥu l-maḥẓūrāt), since combatting need has priority over the inflicting of punishment or other regulations. As I have already indicated, Omar I made use of this principle.

More important than the principle mentioned above is the statement of the Prophet Muhammad: 'Do away with the punishments (ḥudūd) if there is any doubt (idraʾu al-ḥūduda bi-š-šubuhāt)'. So there must be no doubt whatsoever about the correctness of the accusation if the relevant punishment is to be inflicted. Punishments serve mainly as deterrents. If a crime can be demonstrated with absolute certainty, then the punishment must be carried out, otherwise criminals will never take the penalties prescribed seriously.

5. The Qur'an and the problems of historical-critical interpretation

There were Muslim religious scholars who began on critical discussions of the Qur'an and left behind much material for subsequent generations to work on. Most of these works were internal criticism. They were concerned with the internal problems of the Qur'an text. We find external criticism only in works on the miraculous character of the Qur'an (iʿǧāz al-qurān), with which Muslims sought to demonstrate the divine authenticity of the Qur'an.

Contrary to Peter Antes, who in his book *Ethics and Politics in Islam* thinks that there is 'the beginning of a historical-critical approach to the Qur'an only in one respect', in my view the achievements of earlier Muslims are more than just a beginning.

Antes sees the beginning in the division of the surahs into surahs from Mecca (610–622) and surahs from Medina (622–632). However, if one consulted the studies of the Qur'an which were composed from the second-third/eighth-ninth centuries on, one would find many more indications of historical criticism than this simple division, e.g. the *asbāb an-nuzūl* ('occasions for revelation'). ʿAlī ibn al-madīnī (234/848) wrote the first work that can be considered a historical-critical interpretation of the Qurʾan. The most famous example of this kind of interpretation was written by al-Wāḥidī (468/1–76); he was followed by Ibn al-Ǧawzī (597–1201) and Ibn Ḥaǧar al-ʿAsqalānī (852/1449).

The works of the latter scholars investigated the occasion for revelation, the time and the situation, the sphere of validity and permanence of the Qurʾan. There are verses the statements in which apply only to the time in which they were revealed, and others which are valid for all time.

There is also another kind of Qurʾanic scholarship which is concerned with problems of abrogation (an-nāsiḫ wa-l-mānsūḫ). These are commandments or prohibitions which have been abrogated or accentuated by verses which were revealed later, like the prohibition of alcohol and the change of the direction of prayer from the al-Aksa mosque to the Kaʾba.

In these two kinds of interpretation of the Qurʾan we have significant beginnings and foundations of historical-critical interpretation which can be built up and developed today.

The ḥadīṯ sciences are almost exclusively built up on a historical-critical method which strongly influenced other Islamic sciences like historiography.

If the European view matched the account of historical-critical interpretation given here, Muslims would have little objection to it. So I share the concern of Josef van Ess that to speak of the historical-critical interpretation of the holy scriptures in inter-religious dialogue may endanger them.[4]

Translated by John Bowden

Notes

1. Hans Zirker, *Christentum und Islam*, 113.
2. H. Küng, *Christianity and the World Religions*, New York 1986 and London 1987, 28.
3. Angelika Neuwirth, in *Weltmacht Islam*, 70.
4. Josef van Ess, in *Christianity and the World Religions* (n. 2), 97.

What shall be the Answer to Contemporary Islamic Fundamentalism?

M. Salim Abdullah

The first and chief duty of any Muslim is to bear witness that God is one – Islam as a religious community stands and falls with this doctrine. The doctrine can be clad in a single dogmatic statement: 'No one is worthy of worship, and there is no object of love and desire, apart from God.'

For the Muslim, the unity and uniqueness of God is an expression of mystery: for God *is* mystery (2/4), and the believer must worship and bear witness to this mystery which is not revealed and cannot be revealed in its innermost being: 'God, there is no god but Him, the Living, the Ever-existent one' (3/3).

1. The Islamic picture of God

The 'Al-Fatiha', the opening surah of the Qur'an, the 'chief prayer' of Islam, is also called 'umm al-Qur'an', mother of the book, since it contains the essence of the whole of the venerable book of Islam. Like a nutshell, this chapter contains within it all the knowledge that a person needs for moral and spiritual well-being.

The 'Al-Fatiha' begins with God's proper name, 'Allah'. Then follows *rab-ul-alamin*, the most important attribute of God. *Rab* means the one who cherishes, fosters and guides his cause in such a way as to develop it stage by stage – to perfection.

It is difficult to translate this word into a foreign language. The term 'the Lord' is only a rough approximation of it.

We find the proper name 'Allah' 2,800 times in all in the Qur'an, the attribute *rab* about 960 times. The most important names after that are *rahama*, *rahim* and *malik*.

The two attributes *rahman* and *rahim* both come from the root *rahmana*, which means: he shows grace, he was friendly and kind, he forgave and pardoned. *Rahman* is the extent of *fa'lan* and communicates the concept of repetition and the generous rewarding of those who merit it. So *rahman* means that love has priority in the divine nature, that God shows his favour and his grace even to those who have done nothing to deserve it. *Rahman* is a form of intensity. With God there are no limits to grace and mercy. He gives them without being asked and without any merit on the part of the recipient. He bestows them on anyone regardless of colour and race. His sun shines on believers and unbelievers. The clouds pour down rain on all, whether they have deserved it or not. As *rahman*, God satisfies our needs without our having to ask him, indeed without our knowing what we need. He created the universe long before we existed, and ordered it in such a way that we human beings can live in this world. The *rahman* has provided for us.

The second form, *rahim*, speaks of repeated action: God is constantly merciful when this property is called on. In contrast to the first form, the second depicts that mercifulness of God that we direct upon ourselves by our own efforts. As *rahman* God puts the treasures of nature at our disposal, and as *rahim* he hears our prayers and blesses our work.

There follows the fourth main attribute, *maliku-jaum-id-Din* = the sovereign of the day of judgment (the one who controls the day of judgment).

Islam understands God on the day of judgment – on the Last Day – not as a judge but as sovereign Lord, as master. He executes not only legal justice, but in particular mercy. He forgives us human beings without our having deserved it. Indeed he gives beyond the measure of human merit.

A look at the four main attributes of God shows the wise connection between the individual attributes: as *rahman* God has given us every possibility and capacity necessary for the development of the human race, without our meriting it or desiring it. As *rahim* he allows us to reap the fruits of our labours. A God who is *rahman* can and does forgive sins. The attribute *rahim* indicates that God grants us grace and mercy over and above the measure of our merits. Finally, the fourth main attribute reminds us of the day of judgment. We should constantly remember that our spiritual and material possessions are merely loans of which we shall have to give account. This admonition should preserve us from arrogance and self-satisfaction.

However, God is finally also depicted against the background of judgment as a lord and master whose mercy knows no bounds. In other words, the God of Islam is the God of justice – but also the God of love, forgiveness and mercy.

The divine property *malik* is also depicted in the main body of the Qur'an as *al-ghaffar*. This word has the significance of forbearance, forgiveness: the one who cannot cease to forgive.

Together with their verbs, moreover, *rahman* and *rahim* occur 560 times in the Qur'an; then follows *ghaffur*, 230 times.

So it is clear that the Qur'an impressively proclaims the readiness of God, his concern to forgive the sins of his servants, to accept repentance. Time and again the Qur'an recalls that good deeds will be richly rewarded, whereas evil deeds will either be forgiven or have an equal level of retribution. So great is God's unconditional grace that the Qur'an proclaims: 'Servants of God, you that have sinned against your souls, do not despair of God's mercy, for He forgives all sins. It is He who is the forgiving one, the Merciful' (39/54).

The Qur'an gives ninety-nine attributes of the one God by which he wills to be called on. Surah 7/181 states: 'God has the Most Excellent Names. Call on Him by His Names and keep away from those that pervert them. They shall be punished for their misdeeds.' These attributes give believers an idea of God, allow them to have an inkling of his being, bring them near to God in prayer, create an atmosphere of trust, friendship, confidence and gratitude, precisely what Christians describe, for example, as 'being a child of God', in order to express their relationship with God as a loving Father. Here I can mention only some of these attributes:

God is the Almighty and the Compeller; He is the Lord and King; He is the Light, the True, the Just; He is the Guardian and the Judge, the Creator, Maintainer and Sustainer, the Holy One, the All-Seeing, All-Knowing and All-Hearing, but He is also the Peaceable One, the Gracious One, the Benevolent, the Benefactor, the One who hears Graciously, the Donor of Livelihood, the Friend who keeps Faith and the Protector, the One who is Moved to Compassion and Accepts Repentance, the First and the Last.

2. The love of God

The love of God in Islam does not just arise from the deep recognition of being dependent on God. The love of God is above all the fruit of serious and innermost striving to reflect the properties of God in one's own life and in dealing with fellow human beings. Reflection on these properties is the criterion of true humanity and shows how close the ties are between human beings and God, how trustingly God and man relate to each other. By accepting the divine properties into his own life the searcher finds kindled in his heart a fire that purifies him, that compels him to share himself through acts of concern for his fellow human beings. It is this fire which makes the believer capable of consuming himself in devotion to his fellow human beings in God. The one who is caught up in the purifying fire of God no longer seeks praise and reward. Such a person does good even if there is a danger that it will be to his disadvantage, and helps even when he encounters hatred and calumniation. Such a person forgives even when the insults hurled at him threaten to become beyond bearing.

It is a believing Muslim's own experiences with God which make him act as his heart dictates, for he knows (whether consciously or unconsciously) that God is acting through him. The life of one who is immersed in the love of God has emptied itself so as to be capable of openness to fellow human beings, so that God can work through it no matter where such a person may be and what the situation may demand.

At many points the Qur'an states explicitly that God loves those who do good and are pious, patient, just and merciful. And in surah 2/166 believers are described as those 'who are stronger in their love of God' than those who erroneously love their idols. The following passages of the Qur'an speak of the mutual love between God and believers:

Say: 'If you love God, follow me. God will love you and forgive you your sins. God is forgiving and merciful' (3/32);
Believers, if any among you renounce the Faith, God will replace them by others who love Him and are loved by Him, who are humble towards the faithful (5.55).

The initiative of love lies with God. On this the mystic Bistami (803–875) said:

In the beginning I imagined that it was I who thought of God, who knew Him and loved Him. When I came to the end, I saw that He had thought of me before I thought of Him, that He had known me before I knew Him; that His love for me preceded my love for Him, that He had first sought me so that I could seek Him.

It is always God who seeks to make contact with his servant. God leads him on His ways, as the Qur'an time and again makes clear with great intensity. And He makes it easy for him to fulfil his religious obligations. God gives human beings the grace of prayer and comes close to them by rescuing them from the prison of their desires and forgiving them their sins.

3. Is there a fundamentalist image of God?

To ask whether there is a fundamentalist image of God in Islam is of course to presuppose that there is such a thing as fundamentalism within the Islamic community. So first of all this question must be clarified.

As is well known, fundamentalism is a theological trend in Protestantism which over against modern science and critical theology holds fast to the doctrines of old orthodoxy, especially where the literal understanding of the Bible is concerned. This theological trend came into being in the United States at the end of the nineteenth century and took on the structures of an organization in 1918. Since 1948 fundamentalism has been fighting what it sees as the Catholicizing and Communist tendencies of the World Council of Churches.

From this perspective the term 'Islamic fundamentalism' is a further (and, it must be added, a useless) attempt to press certain phenomena in the Islamic world into a Christian mould of thought.

When Muslims, too, occasionally make use of the term 'fundamentalism', they do so only to make clear to their Christian partners in dialogue that there are forces in the Islamic world which would like to stop or even turn back the wheel of history. Moreover, this also applies to the term 're-Islamicization', which has been coined. At no point in time have the Muslim countries fallen away from Islam. So there is also no need for re-Islamicization.

If we want to keep to European terms, then we should use those which have a parallel in Islam. What are meant here are renaissance and restoration: renaissance stands for the rebirth or revival of Islam, and restoration for the attempt to restore former political and economic conditions.

So the answer to the basic question raised here should be: there is no fundamentalist image of God of any kind in Islam, nor can there be any possible kind of re-Islamicization. At present what we have instead in certain legal schools in Islam is the phenomenon of a shift of accent among the attributes which are implicit in the image of God. For certain militant groups it is no longer the gracious and merciful God who stands in the foreground but the mighty Lord of retribution. The socio-political creed *'al-Islam din wa dawla'* has also been affected by this shift in accent. The forces of restoration which are best called 'Islamist' now stress the concept of *dawla*, mission, more strongly than *din*, judgment. In other words, political questions have largely forced statements of faith, religion, into the background.

5. The new *dawla*-understanding of restoration

The forces of restoration in present-day Islam (Islamists) have come together in various 'Islamic movements', some of which are fighting against one another and branding one another heretics. They are at one only in repudiating basic democratic demands like freedom of opinion and conscience, or freedom of belief (because these are Western) and in fighting against a supposed 'Westernization' of Islam, though to a painful degree the spokesmen of these movements have succumbed to Western luxury. Here in particular we can see the ambivalance of these forces.

Furthermore, one of the essential aims of the Shi'ite branch of the 'Islamic movement' is the propagation of the 'Islamic world revolution' and the 'annihilation of the Great Satan' (= USA).

However, it should also be noted that there are agreements between the Islamists and the Reformists. Both wings of contemporary Islam are concerned for the rediscovery and revival of unfalsified Islamic values and thus for the regaining of an original Islamic identity. However, for the Reformists it is clear that these values must constantly be examined against the background of changing times and must be adapted to each new development if they are to be a help to Muslims in life and put them in a position to cope with its challenges.

6. The criticism of restoration by the Islamic Enlightenment

For some years the Islamic Reformists have argued very seriously against the phenomena of restoration and in so doing have come to see the dangers which lurk within the arcane discipline which is implicit in the 'Islamic movement'. They see behind this development a 'degrading of Islam so that it becomes a pure instrument of power and control'. The dubious concealment of the purely religious, moral and eschatological role of Islam which is bound up with this has meanwhile provoked considerable unease among those Muslims who are most conscious of their faith and the problems it faces. According to the Reformists, at present it also seems that in Islam little value is attached to tolerance and respect for the opinion of others. This has led to excessive types of behaviour in the Islamic world and has poisoned the social climate. It is now the order of the day to accuse those with other opinions of lacking faith.

In July 1985 a statement by the Reformists remarked that 'politicized Islam' was a disaster for Muslims in Europe and had brought Islamic faith into disrepute. The old resentments, it was said, had arisen again. The anti-Turkish and anti-Islamic 'historical memory' of the Christian masses found its starting-point confirmed. For European Muslims, according to the statement, the present-day 'house of Islam' has virtually become a 'house of fools': 'On the one hand aggression, and on the other hand talk of the "will for peace which cannot be constrained"; on the one hand the introduction of the Shari'a, on the other, in the same land, scandalous betrayal of Islam; on the one hand talk of tolerance and human rights, and on the other the persecution of those who have been proscribed and other traumatic phenomena.'

The unavoidable consequences of politicization include, it is argued, friction, a loss of orientation, proneness to manipulation, insistence on being in the right, fanaticism, a battle of all against all, a loss of humanity.

In the view of the Reformists the present phenomenon is not an Islamic renaissance but a purely political and cultural counter-tendency which sets itself against alien cultural imperialism and strives for self-discovery among the masses of the Muslim people. The extreme phenomena of this process, which have been called the 'Islamic revolution', are often an expression of social discontent 'which is clothed by skilful manipulators in a religious garb'. By contrast, here there is no real renaissance of Islam in the sense of far-reaching moral renewal, the opening up of new realms for personal creativity and greater humaneness in life.

From these insights the critics of the 'Islamic movement' conclude that the present development is to be regarded on the one hand as an expression of the loss of true religious values and on the other as confirmation of the effect of a large-scale anti-Islamic conspiracy. All those fanatics 'who sow terror and murder in the name of Islam' are consciously or unconsciously involved in this conspiracy.

In September 1986 the 'doyen of Islamic scholars', Muhammad Assad, finally felt compelled to intervene in the debate on reform theology. In the journal *Arabia* he warned the 'Islamic movement' against a total repudiation of Western civilization and its achievements. Were that to happen, the Islamic world would rob itself of the benefits which it could derive from this civilization for its own advantage. As people were learning to use their own intellects in the schools and universities of the Western world, no Muslim should be ashamed of deciding to attend these places of training and education. According to Muhammad Assad, he himself would probably never have gone over to Islam had he not learned to use his mind at European schools.

In this connection Assad also attacked those groups of Muslims who attempt to emphasize their Islamic identities by externals, for example by wearing special clothing. In this way, he argued, many of these so called 'Islamists' had fallen back into a period which belonged five or six hundred years in the past. Moreover, the life-style which they practised could not be attributed either to the Prophet Muhammad or to his companions. Rather, it was derived from the time of the Abbasids and Mamluks, i.e. a time of decline.

6. Encounter as a task

The question of dialogue, encounter with those of other beliefs, encounter with other peoples, races and nations, is a basic question for Islam which is not directly posed by human estimation or human societies. If one follows the Qur'an, encounter with other people must be understood as a part of Muslim identity, as unchangeable as belief in God itself.

The Qur'an clearly states that encounter with other human beings is a divine task which has to be fulfilled unconditionally by both the individual Muslim and society.

The Qur'an envisages three levels of encounter with those of other faiths or other ways of thought. Here it takes Christians and Jews into account on the basis of its understanding that Islam is rooted in the biblical sphere and has to assume the function of reminding the 'people of the book' of the existence of the One and Eternal God.

The Qur'an warns Jews, Muslims and Christians not to leave this way. It seeks simply to bear witness to the unity of God by confirming the pre-Qur'anic prophets. The three levels are: community in dialogue, community in vying with each other, and table fellowship.

Whereas the statements about community in dialogue starting from the oneness of God to some extent express the equality and equal rights of the partner in dialogue, community in vying with one another goes into detail about this divinely-willed co-existence and describes it as a fellowship in multiplicity. First of all we learn that God has given Jews, Christians and Muslims a 'clear statement and a clear way', and then that in his divine counsel he did not will that these three communities of faith should fuse into one. This statement corresponds with another Qur'an text in which the different races and skin colours are described as a miraculous sign of God.

According to the text, our encounter is to be understood as 'vying with one another in good works', bound up with the admonition that God will tell us who among us was just or unjust (5/45–49). Here the Qur'an clearly avoids any denigration of and discrimination against those of other faiths and their communities. It denies human beings the power to judge the faith and convictions of others and points out that judgment is reserved for God, and that to anticipate him in this would be *shirk* (the sin of giving God associates).

With the support of these texts it can be said that dialogue with others, encounter with other communities or forms of organization, is part of divine revelation in the Qur'an and thus an indispensable task of Islam and Muslims. A Muslim who deliberately rejects encounter with those of other faiths and other ways of thinking, or even opposes and fights against them, betrays God's cause. This fact cannot be done away with by the often negative effects of Islam in the world, or by religious decrees (*fatwas*), however 'enlightened' or 'competent' their authors may feel.

The account of creation in the Qur'an clearly teaches that every person who exalts himself above a fellow human being, supposing himself to be better, is an embodiment of the *Iblis*, Satan; they bring down God's curse upon themselves. They have lost the blessing and with it participation in God's honour.

The image of God in Islam is indivisible; the God who is common to us all is unchangeable and eternal. Nor can this image be darkened even by the most extreme and most inhuman happenings. In contrast to the unchangeable, eternal image of God, phenomena are transitory appearances, which moreover cannot represent that which is in itself. That is extraordinarily comforting.

Phenomena are constantly superseded in the human quest for new knowledge and insights. What remains is the 'eternal Islam', the eternal God, who has established it as a message. As we read in surah 5/49:

> Had God pleased, he could have made of you one nation, but it is His wish to prove you by that which He has bestowed upon you. Vie with one another in good works, for to God you shall all return, and He will resolve for you your differences.

Translated by John Bowden

IV · Christian Fundamentalism

The Challenge of
Orthodox Traditionalism

Christos Yannaras

1. Authenticity or alienation from the good news?

For the ecclesial conscience, the word 'tradition' represents a challenge
which is not theoretical but very real: tradition in practice tests whether the
Christian good news is authentic or has been altered and alienates.

It would be a useful way of extricating ourselves from intellectual
schemes to recall here the methodological character attributed by Marx in
his early works to the terms 'alienation' and 'praxis': they are a valuable
means of critically verifying knowledge.

If knowledge derives from the immediate experience of the concrete
relations which human beings have with reality as given, the verification of
knowledge can be carried out only in a negative way: by the attestation of
an alteration of relations so that they become dependence, submission,
exploitation. And if the human subject itself is manifested and determined
through the relations which it establishes, the existential authenticity of
the subject will equally be evaluated as a function of the alteration of the
relations which determine the subject.

I would dare to claim that this Marxist methodological proposition is
ecclesial in the extreme. For it relates to the only procedure which the
church knows for verifying the authentic character of what it transmits as
its good news.

The good news of the church is known in two ways: 1. as an experience
of participation in the relations which make up the 'body' of the church (its
eucharistic hypostasis), relations which determine a mode of existence
which is free within the limitations of time, space, corruption and death;
2. as a word (*logos*) which calls and invites to living participation in this
existential event of the church, to an attestation, only at the level of
experience, of the eucharistic mode of existence.

Thus the knowledge of the Christian good news derives from effective participation in concrete relations or in a call to participate in these relations. And the verification of the authenticity of the relations, of participation in the ecclesial event, can only come about in a negative way, by the attestation of an effective alteration, in other words a heresy.

There are no dogmas – coded determinations of ecclesial experience – before the appearance of the alteration – heresy. That is why heresy itself is not fundamentally an ideological deviation in relation to dogmatic determinations, but in practice the undermining of the relations which form the existential ecclesial event. The term 'heresy' denotes a tearing away and retrenchment outside the relations which constitute the church in fullness (*katholou*) in each local eucharist.

2. Tradition as the expression of an experience

The relations which make up the existential ecclesial event are not vague and abstract. They are very concrete modes, types and forms of action which allow communion with life and existence. These concrete modes are transmitted from generation to generation as the fruit and expression of a communal experience. What is transmitted (in Greek, transmit = *paradido*) is the practice of experiential participation in the ecclesial mode of existence. This experiential tradition is called tradition (Greek *paradosis*) of the church.

Tradition is the transmission of an experience, that is to say continuous communion in a single identical experience: 'That which we have heard, which we have seen with our eyes, which we have looked upon and touched with our hands, concerning the word of life – the life was made manifest, and we saw it, and testify to it, and proclaim to you this eternal life . . . so that you may be in communion with us' (I John 1.1–3). Eternal life is neither a dogma nor an ideological message. It is the historical experience and apprehension of the person of the one who has risen from the dead, Jesus Christ, the experience and apprehension of a concrete existential fact which continues to be realized and manifested in each local eucharist. Without participation in the communion of persons who are learning eternal life, without an immediate experience of this eucharistic mode of apprehension and consequently without the tradition-transmission of the practice (types and forms) of this same mode, of the Christian good news, there is only 'idle gossip' (Luke 24.11), an empty ideological message.

3. Tradition and individual 'convictions'

If the knowledge of the church's good news is the fruit of experiential participation in relations of communion, the transformation of this knowledge into individual 'convictions', individual intellectual certainties, marks its alteration.

The new mode of existence ('eternal life') which is proclaimed by the church consists in the effective rejection of individuality and the realization of life as a communion of love, just as human beings do not derive their existence from nature but from relationships – not their perishable biological individuality but the emptying ('kenosis') of every individual element and the offering of the self in love. 'Whoever loses his life for my sake will save it' (Luke 9.24). The ecclesial mode of existence is a realization of the trinitarian mode of existence; of the eternal life of God who is love (I John 3.16), the mutual compenetration (*perichoresis*) of the existence of the three divine persons. God is not eternal because his nature imposes this on him; God is not constrained to be eternal, but wills himself freely to be living because he loves, and love is his mode of existence.

Thus any human persistence in preserving an individualistic existence is a rejection of the good news of eternal life, a persistence in death. The understanding of the good news as the 'source' of individual metaphysical convictions (of an individual 'faith') and the norms of an individual morality constitute a real reversal of the good news, a radical rejection of the kernel of the promises of the church.

That is why the alteration *par excellence* of the knowledge of the good news is its detachment from an experience of the relationships which form the 'evangelical' mode of existence – knowledge thus separating itself from experience of participation in the eucharistic body of the church. Then the tangible existential event, the good news, becomes an individual ideology, an individual 'religion', an individual morality – but none of that can save human beings from death.

The history of Christianity – a synthesis and reduction of the whole human adventure deployed on the razor's edge of freedom – is also a history made up of alienation and heresies: a multiform perseverance in the death which is opposed to true life. Human beings are thirsty for life, but at the same time reject the preconditions for it: the risks in relationships, going out of oneself, offering oneself in love. The 'fall' of man consists in the human course towards individual existence as a self. Human beings identify existence and life with ephemeral existential capacities of their biological individuality. They derive self-certainty from their individual virtue. They alter their relationships by aspiring to constraint, domination, exploitation, or even, conversely, by their own submission to infallible chairs and authorities which by their recognized weight assure individual armour plating.

In this way they transform the good news of the church – sometimes only scripture, sometimes only tradition, sometimes both together – into an objective 'authority' from which they derive the metaphysical and moral certainties which support their egocentric assurance. They make the church a 'religion', transform it into an established institution endowed with an effective bureaucracy which rules faith as though it were an ideology. The authority of the institution and the weight accorded to the ideology guarantee the individual choice of the 'faith'. Everything functions with a view to providing armour-plating for fallen man, everything contributes towards aiding persistence in death. The eucharist then ceases to be a realization of the gospel mode of existence, a manifestation of true life; it is transformed into an individual duty of common prayer. Dogma, signifying communal ecclesial experience, turns into an autonomous ideological message, into a rationalist code of discipline which protects the individual from ignorance and error. Theology is submitted to the priority of method, restyled as a demonstrative 'science' which offers intellectual certainties. The ascesis of the faithful – the act and the practice of participation in the dynamic of the relations which make up the church – is codified as legal rules and principles of individual moral behaviour. Thus tradition, instead of being the transmission and reception of a living experience, turns into a collection of fossilized formulae of 'orthodoxy', nourishing an individual self-sufficiency which is faithful to dead models.

4. Traditionalism makes the church a religion

In the language of the church, we call 'traditionalism' that extreme tendency to make the church a religion, to replace the communion of relations in the ecclesial body with individual discipline and attachment to given models and codified formulae. The modes of participation in ecclesial communion become autonomous from the very fact of participation and its continuation; they cease to serve and express incorporation into the ecclesial mode of existence. They are absolutized as values in themselves, are set up as idols, as independent 'sacred' data which need to be kept intact and unaltered over time.

In other words, traditionalism replaces the unique and vital functioning of the ecclesial tradition (the transmission of experience through types and forms of action which allow communion with life and existence) with multiple 'traditions' cut off from the transmission of communal experience. The 'traditions' are conceived as being autonomous 'religious' material, objectivized and unchangeable, transmitted from generation to generation as a precious ancestral legacy. The precious legacy must be kept unchanged, not because it concerns our life and the dynamic of our hopes, but because the safeguard itself provides us with good points of individual knowledge, gives us the title of faithful repositories.

Certainly, through time there are 'constants' in ecclesial life: dogmas, moral rules, liturgical order. Nevertheless, it is no coincidence that the first 'dogmatic' formulations of Christian theology (decisions of the ecumenical councils of the undivided church) have been called boundaries (*horoi*) and not dogmas. A boundary signifies a limit, i.e. a delimitation, a determination (description) of ecclesial experience. As description and delimitation, the definition neither replaces nor exhausts the experience but relates solely to it: it signifies the experience. It is the same with the canons which were formulated by the ecumenical councils: they define and signify the presuppositions of the good order of the church or those of the morality of the participants in eucharistic communion without either replacing or exhausting the dynamics of the achievement of good order and morality. Similarly, the liturgical order (the texts used in worship, the composition of the liturgy, hymnology, iconography) serve and express the eucharistic realization of the church without either replacing or exhausting it.

In traditionalism, by contrast, the dogmas, the canon, the liturgical order cease to relate to ecclesial experience, to signify and define it. Each element acquires its autonomy and becomes a value in itself. The dogmas are transformed into ideological principles, the canons into legal dispositions and the liturgical order into obligatory ceremonial. And the individual who 'embraces' the principles, obeys the dispositions and meticulously observes the ceremonial is sure of himself, of his 'faith', of his 'virtue' and his 'piety', even if he remains without the taste or experience of the mode of existence which makes up the church.

5. 'Orthodoxy' is not a traditionalism

In the language of our contemporaries, 'traditional' tends to be identified, at the level of meaning, by the word orthodoxy. Certainly orthodoxy tends more to denote attachment to a dogma, to the letter of an ideology. But in practice it is equivalent to conservatism, to persistence in the inherited forms of a codified practice. In this perspective that person is orthodox who remains faithful to the original and authentic formulation of a teaching, to the rigorous preservation of a consecrated practice, as opposed to those who alter the original authenticity or depart from it.

Thus every dogmatic ideology – whether religious, social or political – has its orthodoxy. People talk, for example, of Lutheran, Freudian or Marxist orthodoxy, intending to denote attachment (conservative and generally sterile) to the formulations of Luther himself, Freud himself or

Marx himself – the comparison of this fidelity with later interpretations or with reforms of the foundational ideas, creative though these later interpretations may be.

Ordinarily the invocation of orthodoxy is made not without basking in glory for having remained faithful to the original and the authentic. To talk of basking in glory is to indicate a common recognition and respect for the legacy of the tradition but also for the people who conserve it and represent it. So orthodoxy comes to function as a means of justifying not so much conservative ideas as conservative people. It often serves to make up psychologically for pusillanimity or spiritual sterility. Those who dare not or cannot create anything new in their lives hold on to an orthodoxy in a fanatical way. They derive a weight, an authority and finally a power from it as representatives and stewards of authentic values – defenders of forms, interpreters of the letter. Finally, they transform so-called orthodoxy into a kind of individual and egocentric armour-plating.

6. Fundamentalism in Orthodoxy

When in the Great Schism during the eleventh century (1054) the pope and patriarch of Rome took the initiative in splitting the unique body of the one, holy, catholic and apostolic church by removing the churches of western and central Europe, he took for these the name of 'Catholic Church'. All the other patriarchates of the Christian 'ecumene' then began to designate themselves 'Orthodox', to distinguish the Orthodox Catholic Church from the Roman Catholic Church.

The designation 'Orthodoxy' thus relates to a specific way of understanding the catholicity of the church. The axis of all the theological innovations of Rome was the interpretation of catholicity as a geographical universality, while the Orthodox remained convinced of the catholicity of each local eucharist. For the Orthodox, each particular eucharist celebrated with a mention of the local bishop realizes and manifests the perfect church, in fullness (Greek *katholou*), and the existential event of the mode of existence proclaimed by the gospel.

When the greater part of the Christian 'ecumene' of the time was subjected to Turkish barbarism (from the fifteenth century on), the ancient patriarchates (New Rome-Constantinople, Alexandria, Antioch and Jerusalem) were for many centuries plunged into cultural silence and a decline in populations. By contrast, central and western Europe, with the 'Renaissance' and then the 'Enlightenment', became the matrix for a literally 'cosmogonic' cultural transformation. Western European civilization (a way of organizing but also of understanding life) thus showed a surprising dynamism and universality and became synonymous with the progress and development of human societies.

The people who remained Orthodox and who struggled to liberate themselves from the Turkish yoke in the nineteenth century were very quickly assimilated to the Western mode of progress and development, or themselves aspired to this assimilation. The radical occidentalization of Orthodox Russia had been promoted at the beginning of the eighteenth century by the drastic reforms of Peter the Great. Thus from then on, the Western understanding and organization of life were also dominant among the Orthodox peoples. The differences of a theological and ecclesial kind which separated Orthodoxy and the West ceased to be reflected in the actual life of people. From then on Orthodoxy was marked out at the level of purely theoretical ideological differentiations and the originality of a particular ritual practice.

The ideological and ritualistic understanding of ecclesial Orthodoxy inevitably leads to an exaltation of traditionalism. That is why even now in Orthodox churches one can see a wealth of firmly conservative movements, regroupings of the true Orthodox. One can see a recrudescence of ideological anti-occidentalism, of fanatical opposition to the 'ecumenical movement' and mistrust of inter-Christian 'dialogue'. These symptoms abound in Orthodoxy today and do not differ essentially from the manifestations of traditionalism which one can equally see in Roman Catholicism and Protestantism. The morphology and typology of the symptoms may differ, but one is struck by the similarity of the characteristics of those who are shaping traditionalism everywhere: the same state of mind, the same psychology, the same stereotyped criteria, the same wooden codifications.

This similarity of anthropological consequences shows the common and basic character of all traditionalism, its real identity as I described it in the opening pages: it is a constant attachment to the egocentric armour-plating of the individual by means of legalistic schemes, ideological convictions and forms set up as idols; it is a refusal to take part in the experience of the communion of relations, a fear of becoming adult, i.e. a fear of freedom, a fear of the risk which offering oneself in love involves.

In traditionalism one can see quite tangibly the reversal and inversion of the boundaries of the good news of the church.

Translated by John Bowden

Themes touched on in this article are developed at greater length in:

John Zizioulas, *Being as Communion*, New York 1985
Christos Yannaras, *Faith through Experience*, Edinburgh 1991; *Philosophie sans rupture*, Geneva 1986; *The Real and the Imaginary in Political Economy* (in Greek), Athens 1989; *Rationalism and Social Praxis* (in Greek), Athens 1984.

A Fundamentalist Pope?

Peter Hebblethwaite

Many scholars claim that 'fundamentalism' cuts across all religious boundaries. Islamic fundamentalism is at work in Iran while a Jewish variety can be seen in Israel. There has been talk of Buddhist and Hindu fundamentalism; and it is true that as world religions emerge from their ghettoes and come closer, they begin to resemble each other, for good or ill. Muslims, especially, often claim that they are by definition fundamentalists if that means a firm attachment to the teaching of the Qur'an; applied to them, the word is a pleonasm.

1. Roman-Catholic fundamentalism and the pope

If we take fundamentalism not as a set of doctrines but as an attitude to religious belief, characterized by the canonization of a text from the past, attachment to its literal meaning and the conviction that a small group is alone saving the world by fidelity to the original inspiration, then Roman Catholic fundamentalists undoubtedly exist. They tend to reject the label because of its Protestant associations.[1] The Catholic fundamentalists differ from their Protestant brothers (and sisters) in that they replace the Bible, which they neither care about nor read, by church councils, especially Trent (as an anti-Protestant council) or Vatican I (as an anti-modern council). Or they combine the two. These councils represent the 'golden age' when 'the church knew where it was going'. Since then it has lost its way, being invaded by secularism, Marxism, Zionism, scientism or freemasonry (mix your own cocktail), which have brought it to ruin. However, fear not, the group is there, guarding the sacred texts, denouncing the present hierarchy in its light, and offering itself humbly as a 'faithful remnant' which will save the church.

However, this approach conveniently relegates Catholic fundamentalism to a kind of theologically irrelevant lunatic fringe, and permits one to scapegoat the late Archbishop Marcel Lefebvre. It would be comforting to think that with his excommunication Catholic fundamentalism came to an end.

David Martin, Anglican priest and sociology professor, cuts much closer to the bone. Though Catholics generally tend to reject the label fundamentalism, he says,

> actually a case could be made out for regarding Catholicism as inherently fundamentalist in that the official definitions offer a complete, all-embracing system. That system does not need to be theocratic in the traditional manner, but there is a strong deposit of the theocratic ambition 'on the books' which has been modified and qualified only quite recently.[2]

Most theologians would be unwilling to defend Catholicism as an 'all-embracing system', but would be hard-pressed to deny the 'strong deposit of the theocratic ambition'.

Pope John Paul II not only embodies but glories in theocratic ambition. His 'insistent appeal to authority' is for Paul Valadier the 'Catholic form of fundamentalism'. The fundamentalist temptation is for the church to hand down *certainties* as though it possessed 'a complete and total answer to the problems of society, and identifies Catholicism as a counter-society or a counter-culture facing up to the bogeyman of materialism, hedonism, secularism, etc'.[3]

So is Pope John Paul the leading Catholic fundamentalist? Yes, if the definition of someone who hands out certainties is accepted. Some French authors have made this the key to the whole pontificate, inevitably comparing the Pope with his predecessor. Robert Solé of *Le Monde* gives a classic formulation of the contrast:

> The time of painful self-questioning, when Paul VI seemed to carry the burden of the whole world on his shoulders, is over; Karol Wojtyla, the tough old mountaineer, carries the church on his back as though it were a Tyrolian rucksack . . . A church of certainties, without doctrinal fantasies. A more disciplined church, with no confusion between priests and laypeople.[4]

Paul Blanquart opens a discussion of the papal 'geo-politics' with the words John Paul used in October 1978 as he inaugurated his Petrine ministry:

> Open wide the doors for Christ. To his saving power open the boundaries of states, economic and political systems, the vast fields of culture, civilization and development. Do not be afraid. Christ knows 'what is in man'. *He alone knows it*.

For Blanquart it is the key-text of the pontificate. It indicates, he says, a religious project – the evangelization or re-evangelization of the world before the year 2000, but it also involves the penetration of the economic, political and cultural structures of society. 'If the Pope has a geo-politics,' complains Blanquart, 'it is not because he is really interested in the world's problems, but because the world needs what he, the Pope, represents.'[5]

This is neatly said. But why should having 'certainties' be a matter for reproach? If we substituted 'convictions' for 'certainties', it might be a matter for praise rather than blame. In any case, John Paul is always declaring that the church 'does not possess technical solutions to problems'. The Pope works in another order: that of legitimizing and endorsing human values.[6] Nor does it seem very likely that history will judge John Paul severely on the grounds that he was too sure of himself. The words at his inauguration Mass will be seen not only as programmatic but 'prophetic'. What looked like rhetorical extravagance may prove one of the most effective political statements of the twentieth century.

2. 'Polonization' of the church

It is risky to speak from the point of view of 'history', and 'effectiveness' is not the sole test. Yet when the historian of the year 2050 comes to write about Pope John Paul II, the *first* thing he will say is that the Slav Pope went home to Poland in 1978, and that this visit had something to do – to put it no more strongly – with the collapse of the Berlin Wall, the liberation of Central Europe and even the collapse of Communism in the Soviet Union itself. He made this contribution because he challenged the Yalta post-war 'settlement'.

This fixed the destiny of Europe for the next forty years, and looked immutable. The Communist regimes of Central and Eastern Europe seemed no less permanent and assured in Poland, Hungary and Czechoslovakia, where the bulk of the Roman Catholics were to be found.

The situation was worse within the Soviet Union itself. The church in Lithuania, where 80% of the population is Catholic, was savagely persecuted, its seminaries infiltrated by agents, its most intelligent and zealous priests packed off to Siberia. In the Ukraine, where there had once been four million Catholics, the Ukrainian Catholic Church had no legal existence, having been forcibly dragooned into the Russian Orthodox Church by a bogus synod in 1946 in what Michael Bourdeaux has called 'the most dishonourable act perpetrated by the Russian Orthodox Church in modern times'.[7]

Since the attitude of the Soviet leadership was seen as the embodiment of Marxism-Leninism, itself an expression of the scientific laws of history, its attitude to religion was decisive. There was no religious liberty in the Soviet Union, and the KGB-controlled Russian Orthodox Church was a government mouthpiece and stooge. It used the WCC to advance the cause of 'peace' and 'liberation movements' in the Third World. The Soviet pattern – tight control of religious bodies through the Ministry of Cults – was extended more or less efficiently to the 'satellites'.

Moreover, seen from 1978 when Pope John Paul was elected, the prospects for change looked slim after the Prague spring ten years earlier. Though the Helsinki Accords of 1975 made hopeful statements about human rights that were taken up by Charter 77 in Czechoslovakia and monitored by Soviet and Polish 'dissidents', they did not seriously threaten to disrupt the *status quo*. Helsinki, moreover, had ratified the existing frontiers of Europe, and therefore provided a further disincentive to 'revisionist' thinking. The *Ostpolitik* of the Vatican was predicated on the continuing existence of the Communist regimes. It was hoped to move from the *esse* of the Church towards its *bene esse* by 'little steps' (to use the Hungarian phrase).

The originality of John Paul II was that he broke with this conventional wisdom and, by challenging it, dismantled it. This, moreover, was the key to his pontificate, its policy, programme and purpose. Countless articles complained of the 'Polonization' of the church. What was really 'Polo-nized', however, was not the church as such but the perspective from which John Paul saw the world. This was made dramatically evident in June, 1987, on his third visit home, when he stood with his back to the People's Palace of Culture in Warsaw. Before him were ranged the massed ranks of the Polish clergy and seven thousand formidable nuns. Looking eastwards, he saw the church as if in a vision:

> The church which is in Lithuania and Belorussia and in the Ukraine and in Kiev and in the territories of great Russia and of our brother Slavs (and also the non-Slavs); to the south in the countries once visited by the saintly brothers Cyril and Methodius during their apostolic service. And in all of Europe. In the American continents which are preparing to celebrate the 500th anniversary of their evangelization. In Africa, in Australia and in Asia, and in all the islands and archipelagos of all the seas and oceans.[8]

With this mental map Western Europe becomes a subordinate appendage, an afterthought to the grandiose Slav-centred international project. What is expected of Western churches is that they finance and subsidize the 'second world' churches; what is expected of theologians is that they do not rock the boat, that they overcome their obsession with birth-control, and that they do not undermine the audacious global project by casting doubt on the authority which initiated it.

3. Incriminating Western theology

Thus the stage was set for the complete misunderstanding between 'Western theologians' and the Pope. There was a *'dialogue des sourds'* and much shouting at cross-purposes. Thanks to the Council, Western theologians had enjoyed a freedom to innovate, experiment and dissent, such as had not been experienced since the Reformation. Among the things which seemed 'no longer possible' was sacking professors and taking other punitive measures.

In the very first year of the pontificate a rumour (judge how well founded) said that since not all theologians worth incriminating could be dealt with, certain representative figures would be selected for treatment. They were Hans Küng (ecclesiology and papal authority); Edward Schillebeeckx (christology and ministry); Leonardo Boff (liberation theology and 'Marxism'); and Charles Curran (moral theology with special reference to abortion and homosexuality). Each of these symbolic figures was 'dealt with' (some more than once).

It was not that, taken severally, their views were deemed particularly heinous or a danger to faith, but taken together they weakened the authority that was engaged on the global strategic project. One cannot go into battle with an uncertain trumpet. In the front-line and on the barricades, discipline is all-important; there must be no breaking ranks; unity is more important than liberty, regimentation than pluralism, orthodoxy than originality.

Those theologians – they were not many – prepared to endorse the papal line were either promoted to positions in the Roman Curia (Joseph Ratzinger) or made bishops in the German-speaking countries (e.g. K. Lehmann, W. Kasper, E. Corecco, C. Schönbrunn). This contributed to polarization, with the majority of theologians like the signatories of the Cologne declaration and the subsequent statements finding themselves in the 'loyal opposition' – though this concept was not admitted.

Theologians found it hard to stomach that their sometime colleagues were now in positions of authority simply by virtue of their office. Bluntly: being Prefect of the Congregation for the Doctrine of Faith does not and cannot make Ratzinger a 'better theologian' than he was in Münster, Tübingen or Regensburg, when he had to argue his case in learned journals and could be challenged with impunity. Now, besides scholarship, he has power and patronage, censorship and veto rights.

Clearly Pope John Paul expected these 'loyal' theologians, now locked firmly into the system, to 'deliver' the rest of the theological community. The Instruction *On the Ecclesial Vocation of the Theologian* (24 May 1990) was the instrument designed to achieve precisely this end. But it failed in that the reaction of theologians was almost uniformly critical.[9] Coming on top of the 'oath' and the Universal Catechism, the Instruction was almost the last straw.

4. Undermining the collegiality of bishops

But it was not only theologians who felt marginalized by this *Drang nach Osten*: bishops too, especially if they were West European bishops, were set aside just as cavalierly. Cardinals Basil Hume (Westminster) and Carlo Maria Martini (Milan) have been successive Presidents of the Consilium Conferentium Episcopalium Europae (CCEE). The fact that they were elected gave them a certain authority; the fact that both were men of unimpeachable loyalty makes the way they were set aside scandalous. Both Hume and Martini, for example, accepted the principle of the 'spiritual unity' of Europe proclaimed by Pope John Paul at Gniezno in June 1979, and always gave bishops from Eastern Europe due place in their deliberations. The equality of East and West Europe was taken for granted.

So when a Synod on European questions was announced at Velehrad in Czechoslovakia in March 1990, it was naturally assumed that it would be prepared by the CCEE. But Martini and the CCEE Secretariat were eliminated from the proceedings, and the dominant figures were the Archbishop of Paris, Cardinal J-M. Lustiger; Cardinal Camillo Ruini, the Pope's Vicar for the diocese of Rome; the Polish Bishop Jozef Michalek; and the lay philosopher Rocco Buttiglione from Comunione e Liberazione who is the *uomo ascendente* (the 'coming man').

The whole constitutional nature of the Synod is subverted by such arbitrary actions. Collegiality is undermined, the role foreseen by the episcopal conference at the national level is reduced to nothing, and instead of European episcopacies we are left with a scattering of individual bishops, many of whom have been appointed, it almost seems, on the basis that they will be unpopular and impose their iron wills on a recalcitrant church (Chur, Cologne and Austria generally). It is demoralizing for existing bishops when they see obviously unsuitable new men joining them, especially when they know that the reason for the nomination is less pastoral need than papal *machismo*.

CELAM meetings at Puebla and Santo Domingo were prepared by CELAM, and the African Synod involves the African bishops. Why are the European bishops treated differently? Why this departure from due canonical procedure? The answer has to be that they could not be relied upon to come up with the analysis of the collapse of Communism that Signor Rocco Buttiglione, who has access to the thinking of Pope John Paul II, would provide. This can be seen by inspecting the agenda for the Synod. Though it may well have been rejected by the time this is read, what it contains is entirely consistent with the great Eastern project described above.

It involves a contrast between a decadent, secularizing West and an East that is heroic, faithful, etc. Just two examples:

> The nations of Eastern Europe have distinguished themselves by the firmness of their faith or their desire for the faith. Eastern Europe has today turned its back on anything that remotely recalls Marxism, even in theology and the life of the church.

> Western nations may have succeeded economically and politically, but are they really examples of progress as regards culture and morality?[10]

A *num*-question, expecting the answer 'no'.

5. Fundamentalist 'new movements'

While theologians and bishops were cut down to size, the 'new movements' that have arisen mostly in the post-war period have flourished. The imprecise concept 'new movements' was much debated at the 1987 Synod on the Laity. The easiest course is to accept the definition given by Bishop P. Cordes, the effective head of the Council for the Laity (Cardinal E. Pironio having been sidelined). The 'new movements' are those which are registered and approved by the Council for the Laity. That includes Comunione e Liberazione, the Neo-catechumenate, Schönstadt, Focolarini, the Emmanuel movement and a few others.[11]

Bishop P. Cordes formulated the theological case for the 'new movements'.[12] He began from the rapid growth of the Franciscan and Dominican movements in the thirteenth century. The friars met opposition from monks, bishops and parish priests, who all felt threatened in their ministry and their income by the 'new wave'. But it was, nevertheless, the wave of the future, and the Holy See, recognizing its charismatic force, rescued the Franciscan and Dominican movements from the bishops and local clergy and heaped privileges upon them.

Cordes maintained, following up hints from Pope John Paul, that today the 'new movements' represent *the* charismatic element in the modern church. 'Naturally' they are opposed by local bishops, whether C. M. Martini in Milan or P.E. Arns in Sao Paolo, but they can appeal to the Holy

Father who will take their side. This has indeed happened, and it explains the favour shown to Comunione e Liberazione and the Neo-catechumenate, despite the gravest doubts and hesitations felt by episcopal conferences throughout the world. The Synod is a Synod 'of Bishops' after all; it was the place where they should have made their views known on these matters; they did so in 1987, and nothing happened.

But the 'charismatic element' in the church cannot be reduced to such 'movements'. This would be an absurdly narrow interpretation of the conciliar doctrine; worse, a distortion and falsification of *Lumen Gentium*. For institution and charisms are complementary. Institution without charisms would be bureaucratic, dead and ineffectual; charisms without institutions might be wayward and unstable. So the reduction of charisms to movements whose leading feature is docility and subservience to the institution is a practical and pastoral error. One might wish to call some of these movements 'fundamentalist'.

Fortunately, it is impossible to impose this view of charisms. The more traditional idea was that 'religious life' represented the charismatic principle in the church. That is what the theory about the thirteenth century said. And one can say that in the twentieth century religious remain the most abiding witnesses to the charismatic nature of the church, and the most effective because they can call on theological expertise and a close knowledge of twentieth-century needs. The Council invited religious families to renew themselves precisely in terms of two criteria: the rediscovered charism of their founder, and the discernment of the contemporary 'signs of the times'.[13]

However, in the short term the 'new movements' – to which must be added the personal prelature of Opus Dei – bask in papal approval, and are encouraged to expand eastwards. In so far as they purvey a similar brand of Catholic fundamentalism to that described at the start of this article, then one can say that Pope John Paul is ready to exploit them for his geo-political vision, but that he is not finally committed to any of them. The next Pope could – I predict will – alter the balance considerably.

The trouble with the pontificate of John Paul II is not that it is pervaded by excessive certainty. One hopes that all Christians can say with Paul, '*I know* in whom I have believed.' Nor is the main problem one of authoritarian centalization – though that does damage especially in the appointment of bishops and the preparation of documents. The trouble is that the pontificate of John Paul II is highly *personal*. Italian Popes have traditionally tried to rule from 'the centre'. Paul VI felt that when he had ex-Abbot G. Franzoni to his left and Archbishop M. Lefebvre to his right, then he must have struck the *via media*.

The exception proves the rule. When Pope St Pius X led the church to the right, and created non-constitutional means of realizing this coup, his successor Benedict XV dismantled the spy-network and structures of oppression, calling a halt to the anti-Modernist campaign in his first encyclical, *Ad Beatissimi*: 'There is no need to add epithets to the profession of Catholicism. It is enough for each to say, *"Christianus mihi nomen, Catholicus cognomen."* What matters is to live up to these names in one's life.' The same holds for 'fundamentalist' Catholics. Their vocation is to disappear, cast out by the force of mature faith.

Notes

1. One minuscule group in the US claims the title 'Authenticists' – they alone possess the genuine faith. More characteristically, other groups call themselves 'Traditionalists', which confuses the issue, since all Christians, unless they throw tradition overboard, must in some sense make this claim.

2. David Martin, 'Observations and a Definitional *tour d'horizon* on Fundamentalism', *The Political Quarterly*, 1990, 130.

3. P. Valadier, *Lettres à un chrétien impatient*, Paris 1991, 26.

4. Quoted by R. Luneau, Avant-propos to *Le Retour des Certitudes, Evénements et orthodoxie depuis Vatican II*, ed. Paul Ladrière and René Luneau, Paris 1987, 9.

5. P. Blanquart, 'Le Pape en voyage: la géopolitique de Jean-Paul II', in *Le Retour des certitudes* (n. 4), 164.

6. A striking example is what *Centesimus Annus* says about democracy: 'The Church values the democratic system inasmuch as it ensures the participation of citizens in the making of political choices, guarantees to the governed the possibility both of electing and holding accountable those who govern them, and of replacing them by peaceful means where appropriate' (no. 44). This goes much further than *Gaudium et Spes*.

7. Cf *The Tablet*, 13 March 1971, 264.

8. This was the homily given on 14 June 1987, at the end of the Polish Eucharistic Congress. Translation by the Polish Press Agency.

9. Cf P. Hünermann and D. Mieth, *Streitgespräch um Theologie und Lehramt*, Frankfurt am Main 1991.

10. *Itinerarium ad Praeviam Considerationem Instituendam*. Synod Secretariat, April 1991.

11. Cf Frédéric Lenoir, *Les communautés nouvelles, Interviews des fondateurs*, Paris 1988.

12. Jan Grooaters, *Le Chantier reste ouvert*, Paris 1988, says of the debate at the 1987 Synod: 'Le discours le moins moderé fut celui de Mgr Cordes. Il fut consideré comme particulièrement aggresif à l'égard des évéques', 131.

13. *Perfectae Caritatis*, 2.

The Challenge of
Protestant Fundamentalism

Miroslav Volf

1. Introduction: the challenge of fundamentalism

Everybody knows an ugly fundamentalist when they see one. He – much less frequently, she – is that narrow-minded belligerent who refuses to accept a world that does not conform to the religious scruples of his pious great-grandparents. He and his friends are angels of light; his enemies are demons of darkness; and there is nothing in between. It would be easy to write a critique of Protestant fundamentalism – not only of its psycho-social character traits but also of its uncritical biblical literalism, its predilection for capitalist individualism and right-wing politics. But would such a critique achieve much more than to assure the readers that the writer is not a fundamentalist? Fundamentalists would certainly not benefit from it, for it is in the nature of the fundamentalist mind-set to translate every serious critique into a confirmation of one's own prejudices; and non-fundamentalists would learn from it only what they knew or suspected already. So I will simply take it for granted that fundamentalism deserves censure and concentrate on the *challenge* Christian churches face today in the light of Protestant fundamentalism.

For decades after the early fundamentalist-modernist controversy, talk about the challenge of fundamentalism would have elicited only a smirk. For the modernist *Christian Century* of the late 1920s fundamentalism had no future: 'Anybody should be able to see,' wrote its editors, that 'the whole fundamentalist movement was hollow and artificial' and 'wholly lacking in qualities of constructive achievement or survival'.[1] Today we know better. Fundamentalism has not only survived, but also flourished. Over the past sixty years it has worked itself steadily away from the fringes of the American Protestant religious scene towards the centre.[2] In the same period, the old liberal mainline Protestant denominations, which had won the battle with fundamentalism in the twenties, have rapidly lost

membership and gradually but irreversibly turned into sideline denominations. A comparable process can be observed in the countries of the
Third World, where conservative evangelical (fundamentalist?) Christians – mainly of the Pentecostalist type – have become the dominant
Protestant force.[3]

Whether we like it or not, *the fundamentalist movement has almost
paradoxically become one of the main ways of transmitting and inculturating the Protestant form of Christian faith in today's world*. It is this
religious and sociological development, I propose, that tips us off to the
challenge of Protestant fundamentalism. Success as such, of course,
proves nothing – at least not in matters of religion. But then
fundamentalism has more than just numbers speaking for it. For all its
nasty features, it is not an unorthodox sect, but still falls within the
parameters of what is recognizably Christian. The spread of
fundamentalism as an orthodox movement and the parallel demise of
mainline Protestant churches require serious theological reflection by
anyone interested in Christian faith as living religion and not merely as a
theoretical edifice. I intend to address this challenge of Protestant
fundamentalism after giving a historical review of its rise.

But before I do so, a terminological clarification is in order. In recent
years 'fundamentalism' has been used to describe any militantly
traditionalist religious movement. I am not sure that this general use of
the term is helpful. It certainly creates confusion by tending mistakenly
to equate 'fundamentalism' here (say Jerry Falwell's Protestant
fundamentalism) and 'fundamentalism' there (say the Ayatollah
Khomeini's Islamic fundamentalism).[4] The term originated in the
Protestant theological controversies at the beginning of the twentieth
century in the United States. It can be traced back to the publication of
a series of twelve paperback books defending the 'fundamentals of faith'
– such as biblical authority, the virgin birth, the deity and resurrection
of Jesus Christ – against 'liberalism' or 'modernism'. The series was
entitled *The Fundamentals. A Testimony to the Truth* (1910–1915). In
keeping with its historical meaning I will use the term 'fundamentalist'
to describe 'an evangelical who is militant in opposition to liberal theology in the churches or to the changes in cultural values or mores, such
as those associated with "secular humanism"'.[5] This definition by
George Marsden, a leading authority on American fundamentalism, is
admittedly not very precise. But then the phenomenon itself is not
clear-cut. I am not thinking so much of the different kinds of evangelicalism with corresponding fundamentalist versions, but of various
possible degrees and areas of militancy. The transition between an intol-
erant Protestant fundamentalist and a gentlemanly conservative is fluid.

No doubt, one can and must draw a line between them – but it takes a fundamentalist to know exactly where.

2. Strategy of resistance

Historically, Protestant fundamentalism was a belated religious reaction to modernity. More precisely: it was a reaction to the reaction of liberal Christianity to modernity. A book by the Princeton New Testament scholar, J. Gresham Machen, which is probably the best expression of the fundamentalist theological agenda, suggests this by its title – *Christianity and Liberalism* (1923).[6] In the historical section of this article I will treat Machen as the 'paradigm fundamentalist'. This might be unfair, in so far as he himself disliked being termed a 'fundamentalist'. As a matter of fact, however, he came to be considered 'the foremost spokesperson for the fundamentalist coalition'.[7]

'Modern inventions and the industrialism that has been built upon them,' claims Machen, 'have given us in many respects a new world to live in' (3). The new world, however, would be unthinkable without a new science. One of the crucial features of the modern scientific method is presumption against tradition: 'every inheritance from the past must be subject to searching criticism' (4). Since Christian faith is by definition based 'upon the authority of the by-gone age', the question arises 'whether first-century religion can ever stand in company with twentieth-century science' (4). For theological liberals the implicit or explicit answer was 'no'. The liberal theological project was to recast the whole of Christian faith by searching within the early Christian expressions of faith for the trans-historical 'principles of religion' that contained 'the essence of Christianity' (6).

In Machen's view the liberal strategy for fending off the onslaught of modern culture was doubly flawed. First, to abandon the 'outer defences' (biblical doctrines) to the enemy and withdraw 'into some inner citadel' (essence of Christianity) is usless, because the enemy will pursue one even there. Modern secular science recognizes no gaps in which Christians can safely hide their belief in God. In the intellectual conflict with science nothing can be gained by making concessions (6). Second, the concessions liberal theologians were willing to make to save Christian faith amounted to its all-out denial. Liberalism is no longer that 'great redemptive religion which has always been known as Christianity', but 'a totally diverse type of religious belief' (2). At the root of this 'modern non-redemptive religion' lies 'naturalism' – 'the denial of any entrance of the creative power of God (as distinguished from the ordinary course of nature) in connection with the origin of Christianity' (2). If the church were to become liberal in this sense, then Christianity would have 'perished from the earth' (8). Coupled with the cultural crisis after World War I, this firm conviction that one was fighting against 'a different Gospel' gave characteristic ferocity to the fundamentalists' holy warfare.[8]

Fundamentalists had a double agenda. First was a spiritual *renewal of individuals*. 'We hope to be able to show what Christianity is,' wrote Machen in the Introduction to *Christianity and Liberalism*, 'in order that men may be led to turn from the weak and beggarly elements and have recourse again to the grace of God.' For it is only the grace of God that can 'bring light and freedom' (16). But Machen was not thinking only of 'light and freedom' for the 'inner man', to use the phrase by which Martin Luther located the experience of salvation. The 'new Reformation' (16) heralded by fundamentalists entailed a moral *renewal of society* through the spiritual renewal of its citizens. This was the second fundamentalist agenda. They believed that the authentic Christian faith alone is able to 'restore to mankind something of the glories of the past' (15) that modern culture with its scientific materialism, ethical utilitarianism, and the threat of political socialism has robbed from it.[9] Fundamentalists wanted to resurrect 'Christian America' – a society held together by (Protestant) Christian values. (This too was what they called 'saving America'!)

Fundamentalists firmly believed that the path to the renewal of individuals and society leads through the *renewal of theology*. Since the 'different Gospel' preached by liberals caused the malaise of the churches and deterioration of society, the task of a Christian theologian must be to reaffirm the 'fundamentals of the Christian faith' (18). Machen's *Christianity and Liberalism* consists predominantly of contrasts between biblical doctrines and the theological claims of liberalism. The Bible extols 'the awful transcendence of God'; liberalism gives the name God to the 'world-process' (62f.). The Bible teaches that 'man is a sinner under the just condemnation of God'; liberalism believes that 'beneath the rough exterior of men . . . we shall discover enough self-sacrifice to found upon it the hope of society' (64). The Bible proclaims Jesus Christ as the divine and human object of faith; liberalism sees in him a human example of faith (113). The central message of the Bible is salvation from the guilt of sin through the atoning sacrifice of Christ, the Son of God; liberalism teaches salvation by human beings themselves from their sluggishness in doing good (117ff.). A 'Christian missionary' preaches salvation of human souls by the redemptive work of Christ; 'the missionary of liberalism seeks to spread the blessings of Christian civilization' (156).

The main impetus behind American fundamentalism is comparable to the driving force of European neo-orthodoxy: it is the critique of liberal theological accommodation to modernity from the vantage point of the rediscovery of God's 'awful transcendence' and God's salvific action on behalf of sinful humanity. The stress on the Bible as the Word of God in both movements is part and parcel of this rediscovery. Yet the way in which both movements understood the Bible as the Word of God was different. Fundamentalists denied the 'presence of error in the Bible' (74), and this became the central tenet of their belief system, the foundation of the fundamentals. Liberalism, Machen argued, is based upon the 'shifting emotions of sinful men' (79); authentic Christianity is based upon the solid foundation of the completely inerrant Word of God. The battle for the Bible will decide the war between Christian faith and its liberal counterfeit.

3. Method of accommodation

Protestant fundamentalism was a conscious reaction to modernity. But only those who do not know better than to listen only to fundamentalist rhetoric could take Protestant fundamentalism simply as a *negation* of modernity. Martin E. Marty, a keen observer of the American Protestant religious scene, rightly claimed that fundamentalism is 'a *very modern* reaction to modernism'.[10] The split-mind of Protestant fundamentalists in relation to modernity can be seen at the surface level, for instance, in their uninhibited use of modern technology, like radio, television and mass mailing. They 'have "borrowed" the technology of modernization with all its bewilderments and used it substantially to promote nostalgic and simplistic versions of the past as models for the future'.[11] For all its anti-modernist polemics, fundamentalism is also modern at a level deeper than just the means it uses to communicate its message. I will point out only three of its modernist features. All three are key characteristics of modernity.

The first is *individualism*. Fundamentalists share soteriological individualism with much of original Protestantism. The point of the Gospel message is to free the guilty soul from the wrath of a just God. Biblical religion, Machen claimed, 'brings the individual face to face with his God' (153). The church is, of course, important for fundamentalists, but only as a means for salvation and edification of born-again individuals. Correspondingly it comes into existence through an act of the will of the individuals who comprise it. As in liberal social philosophy the state is based on a (fictional) contract of its citizens, so in fundamentalist ecclesiology the church is based on the 'covenant' of its members. They espouse what might be termed a 'contract theory of the church'.[12] But modern individualism, which has replaced the traditional organic views of human relations, not only dominates fundamentalist ecclesiology. It is part and parcel of its social philosophy as well (which has never been fully developed theologically). Machen was not alone among fundamentalists in castigating governmental 'limitation of the realm of freedom for the individual man' and extolling 'the great principles of Anglo-Saxon liberty' (10.15). 'Big government' is a part of Satan's plan for the end times. 'Individualism . . . forms the warp and woof of the Bible.'[13]

The second modernist feature of fundamentalism is acceptance of (inductive) *scientific rationalism*. Its penchant for over-simplifications notwithstanding, fundamentalism is not anti-intellectualistic and anti-scientific. John Dewey was certainly wrong when he claimed that 'the fundamentalist in religion is one whose beliefs in intellectual content have hardly been touched by scientific developments'.[14] When they polemicize against some scientific theories (like the theory of evolution), funda-mentalists do it *in the name of science*. But it is a science of early modernity – a Baconian model of science based on common sense.[15] The fundamentalist interest in scientific 'truth' is intimately related to the persuasion that Christian faith, as Machen put it, is based 'not upon mere feeling, not upon a mere program of work, but upon an account of facts' (21). Christian faith has a definite cognitive content which science can either confirm or contest. Religion and science do intersect and can therefore clash; in matters of religion, the anti-intellectuals are not fundamentalists, but theological liberals, who deny this.

The third and related modernist feature of Protestant fundamentalism is epistemological *foundationalism* – 'the view that knowledge can be justified only by finding indubitable "foundational" beliefs upon which it is constructed'.[16] Unlike Descartes, fundamentalists, of course, did not claim to have a foundation that one cannot fail to believe in. The Bible – 'the foundation of the fundamentals' – *can* be doubted, as the fundamentalists' attempts to prove its divine character and truthfulness attest. But the sum of biblical propositions (all of which are true, because they are the written Word of God) function very much like the indubitable beliefs of the early modern epistemologies. The biblical 'basic propositions' are the corner-stone upon which the whole theological edifice of fundamentalism rests; fundamentalists believe either biblical propositions or proper deductions from biblical propositions, nothing more and nothing less. (This, at least, is what the fundamentalist theory claims. In practice, however, they too read the first-century documents through the glasses of their own – or their great-grandmother's – culture. How else could they have come up with an individualistic version of the Christian faith?)

4. What is right with fundamentalism?

Protestant fundamentalism, then, is both a strategy of resistance and a method of accommodation to modernity. The struggle between 'liberals' and fundamentalists is not between 'modernists', who keep up with the times, and 'primitivists', who go back to the Bible. If we look behind the rhetoric of both movements, we will discover that both want to be rooted in primitive Christianity and to challenge contemporary culture; and that both are accommodating to the modern world and reinterpreting the past in the light of the present situation (though fundamentalists are doing this instinctively rather than consciously). 'Liberalism' and fundamentalism represent two very distinct ways of inculturating Christian faith in the modern world. We almost intuitively know what is wrong at the heart of the fundamentalist way of inculturating Christian faith – that is, non-fundamentalists do. The interesting question, however, is what might be right about it, and what challenge Christian churches face today in the light of Protestant fundamentalism.

Fundamentalism can be analysed as a social ground-swell or a political popular front, as an expression of a particular socio-moral milieu. But whatever else it might be, it is first of all a *religious* movement. This is at least how fundamentalists understand themselves. The one place they stubbornly decline to accommodate to modernity is in relegating the religious dimension of Christian faith to insignificance. Conventional Protestantism often operated on the assumption that the 'modern mind' is inhospitable to traditional religious symbols.[17] So 'liberal' theologians engaged in the business of systematically translating these symbols into something more palatable to contemporary culture. But too often translations turned out to be only weak echoes of the dominant cultural trends in figurative speech. The actual result was the exact reverse of the intended one: a complete irrelevance of the reformulated Christian message. For, as Jeffrey Stout observes, 'there is no more certain way for theology to lose its voice than to imitate that of another'.[18]

Fundamentalists rebelled against 'liberal' imitations. They were, of course, not alone in this. But among the Protestants, their protest was one of the most consequential ones. 'The liberal,' wrote Machen in *Christianity and Liberalism*, believes 'that applied Christianity is all there is of Christianity, Christianity being merely a way of life; the Christian man believes that applied Christianity is the result of an initial act of God' (155). Christian faith, in the fundamentalist view, is neither simply a way of thinking about the world nor a way of living in the world. It has important philosophical and ethical implications, but is irreducible to any of the philosophical or ethical fads. Christian faith is above all else a way of relating to the God who created the world and redeemed it through Christ's atoning sacrifice on the cross. This Christian God is the 'rock of ages', and the message about this God is valid for all times. Whatever other noble or ignoble agenda fundamentalists might have had, their concentration on the spiritual message was not only theologically correct but has also proven much more relevant to modern culture than the fundamentalists' critics would have it.

5. What is wrong with fundamentalism?

The God of the Bible as the 'rock of ages' – this is what is right with Protestant fundamentalism. What is *wrong* with it is the way it has formulated and communicated this message – its militant exclusivism. The phenomenon of fundamentalism with these positive and negative dimensions raises a basic theological question as to whether it is possible to talk about ultimate reality and its claims on the world in a non-fundamentalistic way. The problem is real. It is not difficult to see why a fundamentalist – indeed why any religious person – would want to talk about the 'rock of ages' with absolute certainty: if the 'solid rock' is not to be just 'sinking sand' in the end (as a well-known evangelical hymn puts it), then my beliefs about the 'rock' need to be as solid as the rock itself, it seems. The reason is simple: for me the 'rock' *is* what I believe about it, because it is accessible to me only through my beliefs.

But must religious beliefs be *either* 'indubitable' *or* 'unreliable'? These are the only two options for fundamentalists. The third option, and the truly Christian one, is the *certitude of hope*. Because Christians are a people on the way to their final destiny, their knowledge cannot be a knowledge of those who have already arrived. To treat beliefs about ultimate reality as ultimate themselves would be to confuse being-on-the-way with reaching-the-goal, i.e. to espouse an epistemological form of over-realized eschatology. Until we come to see the triune God face to face, we will have to carry our religious treasure in earthen vessels – in provisional beliefs no less than in transient bodies (cf. II Cor 4.7).

The provisional character of authentically Christian beliefs corresponds to the nature of critical thinking. Its results are always preliminary. If I do not want to accept religious beliefs blindly, I can give them only 'interim assent'.[19] This does not necessarily imply a lack of commitment. Because I do assent to religious beliefs, I can act on them, and I can even place my whole existence on the reality to which (I presume) they refer. But since my assent is provisional, I will have to be open to the possibility that these beliefs could prove wrong.

Such an open-ended approach to religious beliefs that is required both by the character of Christian existence and the nature of critical thinking is suited to the contemporary pluralistic setting. It allows a person to be open in dialogue with others, while at the same time to affirm her beliefs with (relative) certainty. It is precisely in this way that Christians should seek to bring the Word of God to bear on contemporary issues. Unlike Israel of old,

America of today is not 'one nation under God', a nation that is either apostate or faithful to its God, as fundamentalists would want it. The United States – along with other modern lands – has irreversibly become a society in which multiple gods claim people's allegiance. In a pluralistic situation various social factors must formulate only fallibilistic (though not relativistic) perspectives on social life. A Christian vision of a good life for society must have the same provisional character that religious beliefs in general have.

The theological task of formulating the Christian message about ultimate reality in a penultimate way seems easy, compared with the practical task of successfully communicating to non-Christians a message about ultimate reality formulated in a penultimate way. It is true, as Philip Clayton points out, that 'nothing inherent in the nature of religious belief requires us to disallow an interim component to religious assent'.[20] There are many Christians who live with uncertainties that reach even to the very core of their faith. But it is still an open question whether they can be successful in transmitting a living Christian faith to successive generations and to non-believers. One thing is certain, however. If they fail in this task, the future of Protestant Christianity might lie with the fundamentalists – with hard-core fundamentalists and with former fundamentalists who have mellowed with time. Non-fundamentalistic churches face a great challenge, then, of finding ways to hand down successfully to others the treasure they carry in earthen vessels.

6. In place of a conclusion

In his famous essay *On Liberty* (1856) John Stuart Mill bemoaned the propensity of religious people toward intolerance: 'Yet so natural to mankind is intolerance in whatever they really care about that religious freedom has hardly anywhere been practically realized, except where religious indifference, which dislikes to have its peace disturbed by theological quarrels, has added weight to the scale.'[21]

Protestant fundamentalists have proved Mill too pessimistic. At present they seem capable of combining vigorous religious commitment with a clear affirmation of religious freedom as a positive good. This is not a small step for people with the reputation of belligerents. Perhaps they will also learn how to formulate their beliefs and visions of a good life in society in a way that recognizes the provisional nature of our knowledge in the here and now. If they do – and manage at the same time to retain their spiritual vigour – they will transform themselves into a genuine renewal movement which can make an indispensable spiritual and theological contribution to the whole church. That they would thereby cease to be fundamentalists would only be to their advantage. And nobody else would mind.[22]

Notes

1. 'Vanishing Fundamentalism', *Christian Century* 43, 1926, 799.
2. For an analysis of the resurgence of fundamentalism after its initial setback see Joel Carpenter, 'Revive Us Again: Alienation, Hope, and Resurgence of Fundamentalism, 1930–1950', *Transforming Faith: The Sacred and Secular in Modern American History* ed. M. L. Bradbury and J. B. Gilbert, New York 1989, 105–25.
3. For this development in Latin America see David Martin, *Tongues of Fire. The Explosion of Protestantism in Latin America*, Oxford 1990.
4. I am not denying that there are common features to Protestant and Islamic 'fundamentalism' (see Martin Riesenbrodt, *Fundamentalismus als patriarchalische Protestbewegung. Amerikanische Protestanten (1910–28) und iranische Schiiten (1961–79) im Vergleich*, Tübingen: 1990.
5. George Marsden, *Understanding Fundamentalism and Evangelicalism*, Grand Rapids 1991, 1.
6. Grand Rapids 1968. The numbers in the brackets in the text refer to the pages of this book.
7. Ibid., 182.
8. See George Marsden, *Fundamentalism and American Culture. The Shaping of Twentieth-Century Evangelicalism: 1870–1925*, New York 1980, 153–95.
9. There is, of course, a strong segment of fundamentalism which preaches cultural alienation instead of cultural custodianship. On the paradoxical tendency of fundamentalism 'to identify sometimes with the "establishment" and sometimes with the "outsiders"' see ibid., 6–7.
10. Martin E. Marty, 'Fundamentalism as a Social Phenomenon', in *Evangelicalism and Modern America*, ed. G. Marsden, Grand Rapids 1984, 56–68:58 (italics added).
11. Ibid., 67.
12. This, of course, is only a *theory* of the church. Just as liberal societies do not actually function according to the contract theory of the state, so fundamentalist churches do not function according to the contract theory of the church.
13. James M. Gary as quoted by Joel Carpenter, 'From Fundamentalism to the New Evangelical Coalition', *Evangelicalism and Modern America* (n. 10), 3–16:9.
14. John Dewey, *A Common Faith* (1934), New Haven 1969, 63.
15. See Marsden, *Fundamentalism* (n. 8), 212–21.
16. Nancey Murphy and James W. McClendon, Jr, 'Distinguishing Modern and Postmodern Theologies', *Modern Theology* 5 1989, 191–214:192.
17. On this see Leonard I. Sweet, 'The 1960s: The Crises of Liberal Christianity and the Public Emergence of Evangelicalism', in *Evangelicalism and Modern America* (n. 10), 29–45.
18. Jeffrey Stout, *Ethics After Babel. The Language of Morals and Their Discontents*, Boston 1988, 163.
19. For arguments for allowing an interim component to religious assent see Philip Clayton, *Explanation from Physics to Theology. An Essay in Rationality and Religion*, New Haven 1989, 140ff.
20. Ibid., 140.
21. Ed. G. Himmelfarb, Harmondsworth 1985, 67.
22. Kenneth Brewer and Dr Judith Gundry-Volf have made valuable suggestions about the style and content of a previous version of this article.

V · Synthesis

Fundamentalism and Modernity

Jürgen Moltmann

In the title we have described fundamentalism as an 'ecumenical challenge'. The answers from the various religions which we have collected in this issue only partly justify this theme, because religions or religious movements which others regard as fundamentalist often do not understand themselves in this way. The contribution by Elshahed from Saudi Arabia is a good example of this. 'Fundamentalism' arose in nineteenth-century American Protestantism as a reaction to Protestant liberalism and is therefore a well-known and world-wide problem in Protestantism, as the contributions by Martin Marty and Miroslav Volf show well. The mere transference of the term to Catholic traditionalism and its late anti-modernism lessen the term's expressive power, because this is a different religious tradition, albeit in the same cultural sphere. This is shown by Peter Hebblethwaite's article. If we speak of 'fundamentalism' in the Orthodox church, the terminology becomes even more unclear, because one can discover comparable phenomena only with the aid of analogies. Christos Yannaras has attempted this. However, at any rate there is the same Christian foundation, and even Orthodoxy must come to terms with a culture which is called 'modern'. The transference of the designation 'fundamentalism' to other religions – and we have only asked the question of the two other 'religions of the book', Judaism and Islam – makes the term completely uncertain and vague. Therefore Jacob Neusner and Elshahed rightly ask whether this category has any relevance at all for their sphere. However, the old Protestant expression has long since become a socio-logical and psychological category in everyday speech, used in an attempt to understand comparable movements from otherwise incomparable religions and world-views. So we must accept the emigration and extension of the word 'fundamentalism' from its Protestant origin as it has taken place. We cannot reverse history here.

What is nowadays thus termed 'fundamentalism' is a secondary phenomenon: the primary religious, interreligious and areligious challenge is not 'fundamentalism' but the 'modern world'. Fundamentalism seems to be a typically religious reaction to the challenges of the modern world, but not itself to be a challenge. That raises the following questions which I want to discuss.

Is fundamentalism an anti-modern phenomenon, or in being anti-modern is it a modern phenomenon? What is the difference between modernism and fundamentalism, and where are they similar or do they stand on the same basis? How does fundamentalism view the modern world and how does the modern world view fundamentalism? Is fundamentalism part of what Adorno and Horkheimer call the 'dialectic of the Enlightenment' and its internal contradictions, or does it point to the world of postmodernity? Can the modern world get rid of fundamentalism? Is it nothing but what Martin Marty has called obstinate 'oppositionalism', or is it preserving in a desperate way a trust in the earth and time which is being ideologically and technologically destroyed by modernity, as G. Müller-Fahrenholz argues?

1. Fundamentalism in conflict with the modern world

The original fundamentalism did not challenge the principles of the modern world independently and directly, but always only their influences on its own faith community. Therefore the picture which fundamentalists have of the 'modern world' can only be discovered indirectly from their polemic against liberalism, secularism and modernism. Fundamentalists do not react to the crises of the modern world but to the crises which the modern world produces in their faith community and their basic certainties.

1. The certainty of faith is based on the firm foundation of divine authority. In the 'religions of the book' this is the divine authority of the primal document of revelation: like God himself, God's word is free of error and infallible. For Protestant fundamentalists, this was and is the Bible; for Muslim fundamentalists the Qur'an is 'an unfalsified, pure, divine revelation which is exalted above all errors' (Elshahed, 62 above). The historical and empirical sciences of the modern world are acknowledged to the degree that they coincide with Bible or Qur'an, but rejected to the degree that they put this timeless authority in question. Creationists who reject the theory of evolution have founded their own 'scientific' institute in order to demonstrate scientifically that the world was created 6000 years ago. That shows that no blind antimodernism nor even any mere 'oppositionalism' predominates here. Rather, fundamentalists are concerned with the infallible and unqualified rule of their 'fundamentals' over scientific methods and results. Only in cases of conflict

is it said that the white wall is black if the divine authority claims this to be so, or that Jesus cannot have had any brothers and sisters because the dogma of his ever-virgin mother rules this out. For Muslims, too, its unfalsified purity and freedom from error is the basis for the 'universal claim' of the Qur'an, not just over all human beings but also over all realms of life. Therefore Elshahed says that the commandments and prohibitions of the Qur'an have a 'rational basis', without giving rational evidence, for this is not a question of accord with autonomous human reason, but rather the total claim of the Qur'anic revelation over human reason. The primal document of divine revelation cannot be subjected to human exegesis, but conversely human exegesis must be subjected to the primal document of divine revelation. Fundamentalism excludes any rational insight into the historical conditioning of its origin and its hermeneutical difference from the changed historical conditions of the present. The content of truth in the primal document of revelation is timeless and need not constantly be interpreted and presented anew, but simply preserved unfalsified. A fundamentalism of revelation does not argue, but asserts. It does not call for insight, but subjection. It is not concerned with a hermeneutical problem but with a power struggle: either God's Word or the 'spirit of the age'. Nor is fundamentalism any retreat or defensive phenomenon, but an attack on the modern world in order to conquer it. It fits into the various contemporary theo-political strategies for the 're-evangelization' of Europe or the 're-Islamicization' of the Arab world. It is clear that even the most serious mistakes of scientific technological civilization do not justify any surrender of human reason and its rational insights. This faith in authority is not just irrational but also anti-rational.

2. The great enemy of any fundamentalism is called liberalism/ pluralism. What is meant is the rise of modern human subjectivity and its individual freedoms: freedom of faith, freedom of conscience and freedom of religion. These individual freedoms from religious ties became the foundation of the modern democracies in the fight for human rights and civil rights. No free world without religious freedom. By 'freedom of religion' is not meant the corporate rights of the various religious communities, but the individual right of persons 'to worship in the church of your choice', i.e. the right to make one's own decision over faith and the right to change this decision, the right to individual entry into and departure from religious communities. Whether a religious community recognizes 'freedom of religion' is always demonstrated by the way in which it deals with its dissidents and apostates. The individual freedoms of modern human subjectivity are a foundation of the modern world. Science, technology, transport and culture are dependent on them. If they are disputed or abandoned, then this modern civilization is destroyed.

However, these freedoms not only enrich but are felt by many people to go too far and to be a burden. Such people find it difficult to make their own independent decisions on religious and ethical questions. So not only in politics but presumably even more strongly in religion there is the 'escape from freedom', the term used by Erich Fromm in his description of the 'authoritarian personality', above all of Germans. The escape from freedom makes possible dictatorships of religious welfare and disseminates the fundamentalist 'certainties' of a religious kindergarten mentality. Through the 'escape from freedom' one's own decision is handed over to a higher authority and thus freedom from responsibility is purchased. But there is no authority which can decide for a person what this person has to be personally responsible for. The extension of fundamentalist lack of responsibility at a time of growing risks from human power heightens these risks and is itself one of their sources.

3. In Christianity, individual coming of age in religion led to the secularization of the state, education and the sciences. Religion was no longer regarded as an affair of the state – *cuius regio, eius reliigio* – but as a 'private matter'. Protestantism encouraged this secularization most because it was the first to stand up for the individual human freedoms I have mentioned. Therefore it also experienced the first reactions, in pietism and later in fundamentalism. Catholicism was confronted with secularization only as a result of the French Revolution. It reacted with restoration, anti-modernism, and most recently the Lefebvre movement. In the Islamic World, Turkey under Kemal Ataturk adopted Western secularization and the separation of religion and politics. But the fundamentalist movements are re-Islamicizing politics, schools and culture, in order to restore the totalitarianism of the Qur'an: 'According to the Islamic view of the world, public and private life cannot be separated and thus secularized' (Elshahed, 64 above). Common to all these fundamentalist reactions to the modern secularization of culture is the attempt to restore the unitary religious state, whether this is 'the Christian West', 'the first nation under God' or the 'Islamic state', and to do so by religious imperialism, since these unitary religious states have a missionary and messianic foundation. But that creates political religions which provide religious motivations for political and military decisions in order to make them absolute and free of doubt.

4. Permanent modernization is of the essence of the modern world. Since its beginnings, development, progress, innovation and a linear orientation on the future have been built into the macro-project of scientific technological civilization. But that requires that supposed certainties shall constantly be made uncertain and traditional identities given up. Elshahed passes a typically fundamentalist verdict: 'Wherever

Western modernity gets a footing, human beings lose their identity, culture, values and norms. Material values take the place of morality and social coherence' (66 above). Jerry Falwell of the 'moral majority' or Archbishop Lefebvre would put it in just the same way. The capacity to appropriate the past and turn it into something new (cf. G. Müller- Fahrenholz, above 20) is blocked off as 'modernist'. How can this development best be brought about? By understanding time in terms of apocalyptic catastrophes and by the expectation of an imminent end to the world. If the end of the world is to be expected in this generation, belief in progress and a concern for innovation are absurd. Improvements in the situation of the world and investment in the future only delay the end, which is coming anyway, and must come in order to destroy the perverse modern world system and rescue the fundamentalists who resist it. The result is the apocalyptic fatalism of the masses on the one hand and neoliberalism in economics on the other: short-term profits, the incurring of debts and no investments: 'After us the flood'. Fundamentalism can also make itself a factor in ending 'this world', in the apocalyptic Armageddon politics of amassing nuclear armaments for the 'last battle', as under President Ronald Reagan in the USA, or in Saddam Hussein's rhetoric of the final battle, when he attempted to talk into existence 'the mother of all battles' in Kuwait. The heightening of the friend-foe relationship in the horrific modern world to a final apocalyptic battle between Christ and the Antichrist or between the true Islam and the 'Satan' USA, the West, apostasy and blasphemy, are part of the phenomenon of modern fundamentalism. Fundamentalism is in fact supposed and claimed to be an 'experience of the end of the world' (G. Müller-Fahrenholz, 16 above). However, what we have here are not just apocalyptically exaggerated anxieties but a perverse wish for death and a macabre will for the end. Nothing is so disastrous as the expectation of disaster. Anxiety about catastrophes brings on catastrophes, because it anticipates catastrophe and does not prevent it.

If we attempt to bring these four dimensions of fundamentalism under a single heading, we can say that fundamentalist identity is an identity which has been threatened, made anxious and uncertain, and therefore reacts aggressively. It is an identity which is uncertain of itself, but defines itself by delineating and denying real or supposed enemies. For a long time Christian and Islamic fundamentalism were anti-Communist. The worst thing that can happen to such a negative identity is the loss of the 'enemy' over against which one has defined oneself. So since the collapse of Soviet Marxism, anti-Communist fundamentalism has found itself in deep crisis over its orientation. Who is the enemy now? Because these people cannot define themselves without an enemy, the 'enemy' has to be found. For some it is the liberalism and materialism of the 'Western world'; for others the economic supremacy of Japan; and for both, with some probability, whether in Islam or in Christianity. Only when the need for an enemy as part of self-discovery ends can there be peace and mutual recognition between the religions, and especially between Christianity and Islam.

2. Fundamentalism in the contradictions of the modern world

The certainty of victory for the belief in progress, the expectation of soon being able to overcome unmodern fundamentalism, has been lost in the increasingly manifest contradictions of the modern world. Fundamentalism is finding more of an echo and more adherents, above all in the modern world. Why? The catastrophes of the modern world are showing many people that something is wrong with this world itself. After two world wars, after Hiroshima and Chernobyl, after increasing destruction of the environment and growing impoverishment of the masses in the sub-modern Third World, it makes sense to take fundamentalism seriously not only as 'oppositionalism' but also in its unique categories.

1. Over against the linear conceptions of time characteristic of the belief in progress, fundamentalism puts the whole of life in the category of eternity and investigates the 'timeless truths' of faith and the 'absolute commandments' of morality. In so doing, it sets itself diametrically against any time which is lost and to be gained. Its own apocalyptic corresponds only to the end of time which the West's technological and military belief in progress has brought about, whether in a possible nuclear inferno or in the ecological destruction of the world. The great alternative to belief in progress and anxiety about apocalyptic catastrophes is the category of eternity, which relativizes the difference in times which modernism has made absolute. The modern pressure towards contemporaneity also becomes relative in the category of eternity. Its place is taken by 'absolute values', which must be put forward unconditioned and unconditionally. Not least in the category of eternity, the hermeneutical differences over the book of revelation become unimportant, because less attention is paid to the nature of the witness than to the content of what is witnessed to. Before the self-revelation of God there is only one time: the present. One can call this position pre-critical, but one can also argue that it is post-critical, a position which Karl Barth advocated particularly impressively. In the category of eternity neither the time of the book of revelation is made absolute, as tends to happen with fundamentalists, nor one's own present, as tends to happen with historical relativists. In the category of eternity the different ties become 'contemporaneous', as Kierkegaard put it. That does not exclude historical-critical research but presupposes it; however, it distinguishes the hermeneutical mediation between times from the mediation of eternity in time.

2. The modern world presupposes the free responsibility of a subject come of age. But who in the modern world can achieve such subjectivity? Only the educated middle class which has arrived, not the poor, uneducated people. The modern world is not a universe but a divided and split world. The First World has produced the Third World, in which the masses are not treated as subjects and person, but as objects and what Gustavo Gutiérrez has called 'unpersons'. In this submodernity today a 'fundamentalism of the poor' is coming into being, spontaneously and without organization, through the rapid expansion of charismatic groups and Pentecostalist movements. Experiences of the Spirit and a fundamentalist orientation on the Bible are turning passive objects into subjects and communicating a sense of personal worth to 'unpersons'. The Bible is the Word of God, and all who read it and can hear have direct access to God without the supervision of church, state and the educated classes. There is also this 'fundamentalism of the poor' in the rich class societies of the First World.

3. Finally, the secularization of culture and the privatization of faith have manifestly silenced faith and left culture to other forces. We need not want to return to unitary and totalitarian religious states, simply because we lament the lack of religious ties in modern society. Liberation theologians and political theologians also want the return of faith to politics: not, however, by the standards of the Christian empire but by those of the Sermon on the Mount. Fundamentalist millennial politics and political theology as dis- cipleship of Christ can both be found today in politics, but unfortunately usually on opposite sides of demonstrations. If fundamentalists are fighting for the reintroduction of school prayers and penalties for abortion, liberation theologians are fighting for the ending of exploitation and the overcoming of premature deaths among the poor from famine. If charis- matic fundamentalists stress miraculous healings of the sick, political theologians stress the liberation of the oppressed from violence. Common to both is a concern to be politically active as a result of their faith, and a recognition of the material components of salvation and its relevance for this world. Even where the two fight each other, there are striking parallels. On the left wing of the evangelicals and the socially-involved Pentecostalists there is already a series of new alliances with liberation theologians and political theologians: in Latin America in the popular movement, in Europe in the peace movement. Opposition to the contradictions of the modern world unites them.

We shall have to live with fundamentalism – against us, alongside us and even in us. The liberation of fundamentalists for openness to the future of God and the world remains a task for theology and the church.

Translated by John Bowden

Against Contemporary
Roman Catholic Fundamentalism

Hans Küng

Martin Marty from Chicago, Geiko Müller-Fahrenholz from San José, Costa Rica, Günter Hole from Ulm and John Coleman from Berkeley, California, have shown in an admirable way what fundamentalism is today. And I have nothing to add to the precise and acute analyses of fundamentalism in Judaism by Jacob Neusner from St Petersburg, Florida, in Islam by Elsayed Elshahed from Riadh, in Eastern Christianity by Christos Yannaras from Athens, and in Protestant Christianity by Miroslav Volk from Osijek, Yugoslavia. But following my Tübingen colleague Jürgen Moltmann, who as a Protestant theologian has made a fundamental theoretical analysis of the relationship between Protestantism (above all in its Protestant variety) and the modern world, as a Catholic theologian I want to take up the remarks of Peter Hebblethwaite from Oxford and make a practical and political contribution, drawing attention to dangers which threaten the catholicity of the Catholic church as a result of a Roman Catholic fundamentalism which is being encouraged by the present pope.

1. The situation calls for plain speaking

No addition is needed to the confession of being Catholic, declared Pope Benedict XV, after his predecessor Pius X had sought to impose Roman policies in the Catholic Church by every kind of 'anti-modernist' repressive measures – the dismissal of theologians, regulations controlling bishops, doctrinal documents, an oath of loyalty for all clergy, a network of secret spies (Opus–not Dei, but Pianum). It was enough, Benedict stated, for anyone to say '*Christianus mihi nomen, Catholicus cognomen*', 'My name is Christian and my surname is Catholic'. Indeed the coinage 'Roman Catholic', which comes from the nineteenth century is a contradiction in terms, 'universal-local'. And of course 'Polish Catholic' is no better.

Peter Hebblethwaite quotes this sentence from the inaugural encyclical of Benedict XV, having previously given a knowledgeable analysis of the present pope's Polonized view of the church and Slav-centred strategy. Eastern Europe, strong in faith, is the centre of the world and Western Europe is a decadent subsidiary region; North America is looked on with mistrust; and there is a concentration on the supposedly more conservative churches in Latin America (against liberation theology), in Africa (against the tendencies to indigenization there) and in Asia (against Third World theologians). The repressive measures of the church against theologians which affected me in 1979 (above all because of a critical article 'One Year of John-Paul II') have reached out to a great many others in the meantime: well-known figures like Edward Schillebeeckx in Holland, Leonardo Boff and Gustavo Gutiérrez in Latin America, Charles Curran in North America, Eugen Drewermann in Germany, but also countless less well-known theologians who either (as so often in Germany) have not been given a professorial position or (as I am informed from many countries) are forced by threats to toe the line or be silent.

There is no point in closing our eyes to the facts: one must speak out plainly. At present we have a clerical dictatorship by a pope who never learned democracy either under Nazism or under Communism and who now, having escaped the totalitarian Communist system, would like to use very similar methods to force everyone in the church to toe his party line – after the theologians, above all the bishops. He is systematically attempting to re-establish the pre-conciliar Roman system by nominating bishops who conform with the system all over the world – often against the will of clergy and people and thus against all Catholic tradition. And he is doing this quite regardless of the costs: a rapid loss of credibility on the part of the Catholic church and its hierarchy, an exodus of women from the church because of its rigoristic and hypocritical sexual morality, the total alienation of individuals, the loss of tens of thousands of priests and an increasingly catastrophic lack of anyone to replace them, which in many parts of the church has now left a third of parishes without a priest. This is a similar emergency to that at the time of the Reformation, though it is being disguised by many bishops with their propagation of what are allegedly new pastoral strategies, as though the hour of the laity comes when there are no priests. In a hospital, who would think of recommending the sick to look after themselves when there are no doctors, instead of bringing in all the physicians who are standing outside in hordes?

Nowadays there are many complaints in Christianity about fanatical Islamic (and partly also Jewish) fundamentalism, and there is too little reflection that the word 'fundamentalism' comes from that Protestantism which seeks certainty for itself and against others by holding fast to the letter of the Bible. But there is also a variant of fundamentalism in present-day Catholicism in so far as its church government is seeking to identify Catholic faith with what are in fact the latest of church traditions (Trent, Vatican I, pre-conciliar papal documents) and to force Catholics back into a mediaeval, Counter-Reformation, antimodernist paradigm of church and society with a 're-evangelization' = 're-Catholicization' – neglecting and excluding ('marginalizing') the Protestants, Orthodox, the Jews and the 'unbelievers'. This is a Catholic fundamentalism with extremely dubious consequences, particularly if one looks at Poland, which is also the unacknowledged papal model for a 're-evangelization' of other countries.

2. The re-Catholicization campaign in Poland

Indeed the current anti-modern 're-Catholicization campaign' in Poland (which is also anti-Reformation and anti-Orthodox) is a striking example of the present Roman Catholic fundamentalism. Since the changes there – according to surveys – the Catholic Church has become the most powerful (but not the most popular) institution, more powerful than the government, president, parliament, army and Solidarity. 74% of Poles now think that the political role of the church is too great. But with this power – especially over parliamentary deputies, anxious about being re-elected – the church has begun energetically to restore the mediaeval *status quo*, so that there are loud complaints not only from Orthodox and Protestant Christians and Jews, but also from open Catholics (like the former Prime Minister Tadeusz Mazowiecki) and also the famous composer Krysztof Penderecki and the no less famous writer Stanislav Lem:

– By-passing parliament, religious instruction has been introduced in Polish schools, which is to be given by a clergy which has had no kind of pedagogical training for it.

– Although 59% of Poles are in support of at least a limited legalization of the termination of pregnancy, one of the most rigorous anti-abortion laws in the world (with two years in prison for women and doctors who practise abortions) has been introduced even in cases of rape, genetic damage to the embryo, and the sickness of the mother (the only exception is when her life is in danger).

– State subventions for contraceptive pills have been abolished (despite the horrific number of abortions each year), so that many women will no longer be able to buy pills, now that they are three times as expensive as they were.

– New laws are also expected against divorce, pornography and much else.

– The rank of general has been introduced for the senior military chaplain, and the church hierarchy are now usually present at important public ceremonies.

– Many bishops are calling for the abolition of the article in the constitution which separates church and state.

– Psychological terror is often being used against dissenters at a local level (for example, those calling for a referendum on the abortion law), and the influence of the church on elections and politicians is growing steadily.

'Church, church over all'? That is what people are writing on the wall. What people? Those who fear a clerical state that will be ruled in accordance with the dictates of the Polish messiah pope. But because since the shift to democracy the church has all too rapidly changed from being a political, powerless haven of freedom to an authoritarian fortress of power, its credibility has been rapidly declining (from 83% in 1990 to 58% in April 1991). A general polarization of Polish society threatens. This process was encouraged by the papal visit in June 1991, in which Karol Wojtyla travelled through his country in the style of a clenched-fist crusading pope and (to the scandal of all Democrats) challenged the right of parliament to pass a liberal abortion law. To the scandal of the Jews, he compared the abortion of embryos with Auschwitz and finally – having in effect affirmed a total pacifism in the Gulf War – praised national political heroism with tens of thousands of soldiers and now affirmed 'the legitimate right to defence'. By contrast, the pope did not devote a single word to the question of an authentic parliamentary democracy.

What particularly stirred the pope was a national survey on the eve of his visit: he doubtless knew about it, though the Polish media maintained almost complete silence on it, and far too little attention was paid to it in the Western press. It showed abundantly clearly what new fronts have formed in post-Communist Poland. To the question whether the Catholic Church has the right to compel people to submit to its teaching, 81% of all Poles replied 'certainly not' or 'probably not' over contraception. 71% gave the same answer over abortion, 61% over pre-marital or extra-marital relationships, and 63% over divorce. And over abortion, even 62% of Poles living in the country replied 'probably not' or 'certainly not'. This figure rose to 81% in cities with more than 500,000 inhabitants, like Lodz, Warsaw and even Krakow. Such figures show that on these disputed questions the church hierarchy in Poland in no way has the majority of the population behind it. Certainly it should not simply give way to the spirit of the time and tacitly tolerate permissiveness. But it would be well advised to rethink its rigorous and sweeping teaching, particularly in matters of sexual morality. Otherwise it risks forfeiting the credibility which it urgently needs for the real spiritual renewal of this land. Those who are

alienated from ordinary men and women on these questions can hardly
expect to be followed on other vitally important issues.

3. The wretched situation over birth control

Now in his most recent social encyclical *Centesimus Annus* (May 1991),
the pope has also attempted to enlighten the whole world on present-day
social distress. At the same time he is using the practices of the Inquisition
to muzzle the representatives of Latin-American liberation theology. He is
noting with satisfaction the downfall of the Marxist systems of the East,
and is rightly criticizing the excesses of capitalism and all forms of
exclusion and exploitation, especially in the Third World. But cheap
criticism of the 'materialistic and consumerist' West, which does not cost
anything, and the regaining of ground in Eastern Europe by exploiting the
situation, is not real spiritual renewal.

As for the Third World, the church's *magisterium* is making itself an
accomplice in the mass misery, the hunger and the death of millions upon
millions of children throughout the world in continuing its worldwide
campaign against birth control (and more recently also against condoms in
the fight against AIDS). Like many of his predecessors since the days of
Luther, Galileo and Darwin, does not this pope, too – blinded by the
doctrine of infallibility in matters of faith and morality – realize that here he
is trapped in error? In this way he is becoming one of those chiefly
responsible for the uncontrollable population explosion and thus also the
wretchedness of children in Latin America, Africa and other countries of
the South. Incapable of self-criticism, he fails to understand that it is a
contradiction in terms to fight against abortion and contraception at the
same time, when contraception could be the most effective way of bringing
down abortion rates, which are in any case too high. At 600,000 per year,
Poland has the highest abortion rate in Europe, because abortion has
become the main method of birth control. This is for want of con-
traceptives of any kind, all of which are repudiated by the pope and the
hierarchy.

But the pope will not understand that it does little help to call for human
rights (freedom of thought, speech, teaching and religion) now, all of
which his anti-democratic predecessor Leo XII, whom he so reveres,
condemned a century ago, when for millions of people, particularly in the
Third World, a worthwhile human life is *a priori* impossible. It is
impossible because the number of people in the pre-industrial, poor,
Third World, who already make up two-thirds of humankind, is increasing
at such a hectic pace that there is no way in which the human investment
needed can keep up any longer. About the time of Christ's birth, around

200 million people were living on our earth; at the time of the discovery of America 500 million; in the middle of the eighteenth century 700 million. With the Industrial Revolution, as early as 1830 the figure topped the billion mark; it doubled in 1925 to two billion and again doubled as early as 1975 to four billion. According to the figures in the annual UN demographic report published in May 1991, there are now 5.4 billion people on this planet. By the end of our century this will already be 6.4 billion, and in the year 2025 already 8.5 billion. Since Paul VI's unfortunate 1968 encyclical *Humanae Vitae* against contraception, the population has risen from 3.5 billion to 5.4 billion. John Paul II has learned nothing from this. In his encyclical *Centesimus Annus* he simply keeps silent on this fundamental human problem.

Though countless people do not have basic food, water and energy, let alone homes, jobs and health-care organizations, and the environment is increasingly being destroyed by the great cities and slums which are mushrooming, certainly there is no case for compulsory birth control measures. But family planning must be striven for by all legitimate political means and relevant social measures (a change in the role of women); here there can be no more effective support than that of the religions. For in the countries of the so-called Third World the religions often reach people's heads and hearts more than great political campaigns. Without the support of the religious authorities, the peoples of these lands will not change the moral behaviour which the religions have instilled in them over the centuries.

4. The betrayal of the Council

The implementation of authoritarian Roman Catholic fundamentalism goes hand in hand with a betrayal of the Second Vatican Council in spirit and in letter. Indeed anxiety about a development of the theological and pastoral approaches of the Council might be a decisive cause of the present fundamentalism.

Already as a bishop, Karol Wojtyla was close to the reactionary Catholic secret association Opus Dei. Was he and is he a member? There is no evidence of this. However, what is certain is that Karol Wojtyla is stamped through and through with the ideology of the 'Slavonic Pope', who according to the myth of nineteenth-century Polish messianism will rescue and renew the decadent church. Thus commissioned by God, in Slavonic messianism he seems to have no bounds to his office and his competence (which exegetically, historically and theologically is in fact extremely limited), and no scruples in dealing with his Catholic opponents, even if these are bishops or cardinals.

However, it is now becoming increasingly clear even to his admirers what the Roman fundamentalist intention of the pope was right from the beginning, despite all assertions to the contrary. A brake is to be put on the conciliar movement, the reform within the church is to be stopped, ecumenical understandings with the Eastern churches, Protestants and Anglicans are to be blocked, and the dialogue with the modern world is again to be replaced more with one-sided teaching. A sign of the change in climate is that John XXIII – who is made responsible for the decline of the power of the Curia after the Council – is hardly mentioned. Instead, there are efforts to achieve the beatification of Pope Pius IX, the pope responsible for the decree on infallibility, who is controversial in every respect, and – as early as 1992 – that of the Spanish founder of Opus Dei.

Granted, both John Paul II and his inquisitor Cardinal Ratzinger made an emphatic appeal to Vatican II. But rather than all the 'fanaticism' over the Council, by that both mean the 'true Council', which does not mark a new beginning but simply stands in continuity with the past. Here what are undeniably the conservative passages of the historical Second Vatican Council, demanded by the curial group (the *nota praevia* on papal privileges were formally forced on the Council by Paul VI), are firmly interpreted in a retrogressive sense, and the forward-looking, epoch-making new beginnings are passed over at decisive points. Instead of the words of the conciliar programme we have once again the slogans of a renewed authoritarian *magisterium*:

– instead of 'aggiornamento' in the spirit of the gospel we now again have traditional 'Catholic doctrine';

– instead of the 'collegiality' of the Pope with the bishops we again have a tight Roman centralism;

– instead of 'openness' to the modern world we again increasingly have accusations, complaints and laments over alleged 'assimilation';

– instead of 'ecumenism' we again have a stress on all that is narrowly Roman Catholic;

– there is no longer any talk of the difference between the church of Christ and the Roman Catholic Church, between the substance of the doctrine of faith and the linguistic and historical garb in which it is expressed, of a 'hierarchy of truths'.

In all this, the Vatican is not just floating like a cork on the waves of a worldwide conservative movement. Rather, this represents a very active political effort. And it is all regardless of the disappointment and frustration at the grass roots. Even the most modest desires within Catholicism or in the ecumenical movement, say of the German, Austrian and Swiss synods (who have worked for years with a good deal of idealism and with the expenditure of a great deal of personal effort, time, paper and finance), are decided against by an arrogant Curia which does not give any reasons: just accept it – the rest is none of your business. The number of churchgoers, baptisms and marriages in church is steadily dropping. Some people – a declining number – keep paying church tax only so as to be buried by the church.

The Roman legalism, clericalism and triumphalism so vigorously criticized by the Council bishops is enjoying a happy resurrection – cosmetically rejuvenated and in modern garb: above all in the 'new' canon law (CIC) which, contrary to the intentions of the Council, sets virtually no limits to the exercise of power by the pope, Curia and nuncios. Indeed it reduces the status of ecumenical councils, gives conferences of bishops only in an advisory capacity, keeps the laity completely dependent on the hierarchy, and completely neglects the ecumenical dimension. This church 'law' is turned into utterly practical politics, even during the frequent absence of the pope, by his Curia, through a flood of new documents, ordinances, admonitions and instructions: from decrees about heaven and hell to the highly ideological rejection of the ordination of women, the prohibition of lay preaching (now, even that by theologically trained pastoral workers, men and women), the ban on women servers at the altar; from direct interventions by the Curia in the major orders (the choice of the Jesuit General, the statutes for the Carmelite sisters, inquisitorial visitations of the American congregations of sisters) to the notorious disciplinary actions against theologians.

So the chain of contradictions is never ending:

– constant talk about human rights, but no practical justice for theologians and sisters in orders;

– vigorous protests against discrimination in society, but practical discrimination within the church, particularly against women;

– a long encyclical on mercy, but no practice of mercy towards the divorced and married priests (c. 70,000, 7,000 of them in Germany alone).

5. How is fundamentalism to be dealt with?

Indeed, what is to be done in the face of fundamentalism in *all* religions? In this issue there is an illuminating agreement between the highly constructive contributions of the rabbi Samuel Karff (Houston, Texas) and the Muslim Salim Abdullah (Soest, Germany) on the one hand and the Christian theologian Geiko Müller-Fahrenholz (San José, Costa Rica) on the other, that fundamentalism can be overcome only with understanding and empathy.

If I am to make a summary, four points seem to me to be important:

(*a*) Fundamentalists should be made aware of the roots of freedom, pluralism, and openness to others in each of their traditions: in the Hebrew Bible and the Talmud, in the New Testament and church tradition, in the Qurʾan and in the Sunna.

(*b*) But progressives must also be made aware of the need for self-criticism in the face of any lazy adaptation to the Spirit of the time which cannot say no; in the face of any lack of religious substance, theological profile and binding ethics in a modern liberal form of religion which knows no bounds.

(*c*) A new basic spiritual orientation must be striven for and lived out credibly, particularly by all those who are not content with Roman Catholic authoritarianism, Protestant biblicism, Orthodox traditionalism, or a fundamentalism of Jewish or Muslim origin;

(*d*) Despite all the difficulties and opposition, dialogue must also be sought with fundamentalists and collaboration be striven for in both politics and social issues, and religion and theology.

However, there is one question which we cannot avoid. What is to be done when fundamentalism is allied with political, military and police powers (in some Islamic states, in the Salman Rushdie affair) or even with clerical power (the Vatican against theologians, bishops, women)? Here, resolute resistance must be offered, both from outside and from within. One example of this resistance is the Cologne Declaration by 163 German- speaking theologians against the Vatican nominations of bishops, restrictions on theologians and claims by the *magisterium*, a declaration which has also been taken up by other international conferences of theologians.

I hope that in time the Catholic church, like other great religions, will find a way between a modernism without foundations and a fundamentalism without modernity, without self-criticism, tolerance and a readiness for dialogue, a way between permissiveness and exclusiveness, between laxity and aggressiveness. I end with the words of the final passage of the Cologne Declaration.

– The church stands in the service of Jesus Christ. It must resist the permanent temptation to misuse its gospel of God's justice, mercy and faithfulness by claiming questionable forms of rule for its own power. It was understood by the Council as the wandering people of God and the living relationship of believers (*communio*); it is not a beleaguered city which builds up its fortresses and defends them harshly inside and out.

– We share various anxieties about the church in our present-day world with the pastors of the church, on the basis of our common testimony. To protect the poor churches, to lead the rich churches out of entanglements and to encourage the unity of the church are aims which we understand and to which we dedicate ourselves.

– However, theologians who are in the service of the church also have the duty to express criticism openly if the church *magisterium* uses its power wrongly so that it contradicts its aims, endangers steps to ecumenism, and goes back on the openness of the Council.

– The pope claims the office of unity. So it is his office to bring people together in cases of conflict, as he did to excess in the case of Marcel Lefebvre and his followers, despite the fundamental way in which they put his *magisterium* in question. It is not his office to intensify secondary conflicts without any attempt at dialogue, to make a one-sided magisterial decision on them and to make them a cause for exclusion. When the pope does something which is not his office to do, he cannot call for obedience in the name of Catholicity. Then he must expect opposition.

Translated by John Bowden

This declaration, initiated by the Tübingen theologians Norbert Greinacher and Dietmar Mieth, both members of the editorial committee of *Concilium*, along with a first group of signatories, was signed by 162 Catholic professors of theology in the German-language area and in the Netherlands. Similar declarations followed in Belgium, France, Spain, Italy, Brazil and the United States. In addition, the declaration was signed in the Netherlands by about 17,000 and in West Germany by around 16,000 pastors and laity and by about 100 Catholic groups.

There is a precise discussion of the problems connected with infallibility which are expressed in the declaration by Herbert Haag, in his preface to the new German edition of my book *Infallible?*, Munich 1989, which has a new subtitle, 'An Unresolved Question'.

For the present situation in the Catholic church cf. N. Greinacher and H. Küng, *Katholische Kirche -wohin? Wider den Verrat am Konzil*, Munich 1986.

How urgent the problem of fundamentalism has become in contemporary Catholicism is evident from the increasing number of books being published:

J. Niewiadomski (ed.), *Eindeutige Antworten? Fundamentalistische Versuchung in Religion und Gesellschaft*, Thaur 1989

K. Kienzler (ed.), *Der neue Fundamentalismus. Rettung oder Gefahr für Gesellschaft und Religion? Schriften der Katholischen Akademie in Bayern*, Düsseldorf 1990

T. F. O'Meara, *Fundamentalism: A Catholic Perspective*, New York 1990

R. Schermann (ed.), *Wider den Fundamentalismus*, Sauerbrunn 1990

W. Beinert (ed.), *Katholischer Fundamentalismus. Häretische Gruppen in der Kirche*, Regensburg 1991

H. Hemminger (ed.), *Fundamentalismus in der verweltlichten Kultur*, Stuttgart 1991

G. Kepel, *La Revanche de Dieu. Chrétiens, juifs et musulmans à la reconquête du monde*, Paris 1991

H. Kochanek (ed.), *Die verdrängte Freiheit. Fundamentalismus in den Kirchen*, Freiburg 1991

J. Werbick (ed.), *Offenbarungsanspruch und fundamentalistische Versuchung?*, Freiburg 1991

S. H. Pfürtner, *Fundamentalismus. Die Flucht ins Radikale*, Freiburg 1991

Contributors

MARTIN E. MARTY is the Fairfax M. Cone Distinguished Service Professor of the History of Modern Christianity at the University of Chicago, senior editor of *The Christian Century*, and director (with R. Scott Appleby) of The Fundamentalism Project, sponsored by the American Academy of Arts and Sciences. He has just published *The Noise of Conflict*, successor to *The Irony of It All*; these are the first two volumes of his projected four volume *Modern American Religion*. Chicago will publish five volumes of Marty-Appleby edited works on fundamentalism; the first has appeared as *Fundamentalisms Observed*.

GEIKO MÜLLER-FAHRENHOLZ is a Lutheran pastor. He was born in 1946 and studied Protestant theology in the University of Tübingen and Yale University Divinity School. After his doctorate in Tübingen he became Executive Secretary of the World Council of Churches in Geneva and later Director of the North Elbe Protestant Academy. At present he is Professor of Peace Ethics and Ecumenical Theology in Costa Rica.

GÜNTER HOLE is Medical Director of the Psychiatric Hospital in Weissenau, Germany and Professor of Psychiatry in the University of Ulm. His main fields of research are depressions and the psychopathology of religion.

JOHN COLEMAN SJ was born in San Francisco in 1937. He holds advanced degrees in sociology from the University of California, Berkeley, and did advanced study in theology at the University of Chicago. He has written or edited more than ten books, chief of which is *An American Strategic Theology*. He serves as editor-in-chief for the Isaac Haecker Series in American culture and religion published by Paulist Press in the USA. He is currently Professor of Religion and Society at the Graduate Theological Union in Berkeley, California.

JACOB NEUSNER was born in the United States in 1928 and studied at Harvard, the Jewish Theological Seminary of America and Columbia University, before going on to Lincoln College, Oxford, for further research. From 1968 he was Professor of Religious Studies at Brown University, and is now Graduate Research Professor of Humanities and Religious Studies at the University of South Florida, Tampa. He is the distinguished author of a wealth of books on Judaism and has made a new translation of the Mishnah.

SAMUEL E. KARFF was born in Philadelphia, and after graduating from Harvard was ordained rabbi at Hebrew Union College, Cincinnati, in 1956, where he gained his doctorate. After serving congregations in Chicago and Houston, since 1975 he has been Senior Rabbi of Beth Israel, Texas' oldest synagogue. He has taught at the University of Notre Dame and Chicago Divinity School and is currently a Lecturer in Jewish Thought at Rice University. He is author of *Agada: The Language of Jewish Faith* (1980), and 'Judaism' in the textbook *Religions of the World*, as well as of numerous articles. He is a former President of the Central Conference of American Rabbis.

ELSAYED ELSHAHED was born in Egypt in 1945 and studied philosophy, psychology and sociology at a college in Cairo before lecturing in philosophy in Aswan. In 1972 he went to West Germany to study, gaining his MA from Tübingen and his PhD from Saarbrücken in oriental studies, philosophy and theology. In 1983–84 he lectured in Islamics at Frankfurt and now teaches at the Imam University, Riyadh, Saudi Arabia. His works include *Das Problem der sinnlichen Wahrnehmung*, Berlin 1983, and works in Arabic on Christian-Muslim dialogue and Islamic thought.

MUHAMMAD S. ABDULLAH was born in 1931 and is a journalist specializing in the history of Islam in Germany and in Christian-Muslim dialogue. He has been a representative of the Islamic World Congress, since 1964 in Germany and since 1988 at the United Nations; he is also a member of the executive council of the Congress in Karachi. He is the author of numerous books and articles, including *Moslems unter uns* (1974), *Geschichte des Islams in Deutschland* (1981) and *Islam – kurzgefasst für Entwicklungshelfer* (1981), and has collaborated in the most recent German translation of the Qur'an (1987).

CHRISTOS YANNARAS was born in Athens in 1935, and is professor of philosophy at the Institute of Political Sciences in Athens. He has taught Orthodox theology and Byzantine philosophy at the Institutes of Orthodox Theology and Ecumenical Studies and in the Protestant Faculty of Theology in Geneva. His publications include *De l'absence et de l'inconnaissance de Dieu*, *Person und Eros*, and in Greek: *The Metaphysic of the Body*, *The Crisis of Prophecy*, *Introduction to Philosophy*, *Chapters in Political Theology*, *The Privilege of Despair* and *The Unity and Truth of the Church*.

PETER HEBBLETHWAITE is a writer who lives in Oxford, England. He studied philosophy in France in the days of Jean-Paul Sartre, took a First in Mediaeval and Modern Languages at Oxford University, and read theology at Heythrop College, then in rural Oxfordshire. His first book was on *Georges Bernanos* (1965). In 1965 he was in Rome for the final session of the Council and wrote *The Council Fathers and Atheism* (1967). After editing the Jesuit review *The Month* until 1974, he parted company with the Jesuits in friendly fashion. Since then his books include *The Runaway Church* (1975); *Christian–Marxist Dialogue and Beyond* (1977); *The Year of Three Popes* (1978); *The New Inquisition* (1980); *Introducing John Paul II, the Populist Pope* (1982); *John XIII, Pope of the Council* (1984); *In the Vatican*, (1987); he is completing *Paul VI, the First Modern Pope*.

Miroslav Volf is Associate Professor of Systematic Theology at Fuller
Theological Seminary, Pasadena, California and teaches Theology and Ethics
at Evangelical Theological Faculty, Osijek, Yugoslavia. He was born in
Yugoslavia in 1956 and studied theology and philosophy in his native country, in
the United States and Germany. He holds a doctorate in theology from the
Evangelical-Theological Faculty in Tübingen. Until recently he was the editor
of and a regular contributor to a Croatian Christian monthly, *Izvori*. He has
published numerous scholarly articles, mainly on political and economic
theology and ecclesiology. His books include *Zukunft der Arbeit – Arbeit der
Zukunft. Der Arbeitsbegriff bei Karl Marx und seine theologische Wertung*.
Munich and Mainz 1988; *Work in the Spirit. Toward a Theology of Work*, New
York 1991. He is a member of the Evangelical Church of Yugoslavia.

Jürgen Moltmann was born in Hamburg in 1926 and is a member of the
Evangelical-Reformed Church. He studied at Göttingen, was professor at the
Kirchliche Hochschule Wuppertal from 1958–63, at Bonn from 1963–67, and
now holds a chair for systematic theology at Tübingen. He is president of the
Gesellschaft für Evangelische Theologie. His publications include:
Prädestination und Perseveranz (1961), *Theologie der Hoffnung*, 12th ed. 1985
(ET *Theology of Hope*, 10th ed. 1983); *Perspektiven der Theologie*, 1968 (ET
[selections] *Hope and Planning*, 1971); *Der Mensch*, 4th ed. 1979 (ET *Man*,
1974); *Die ersten Freigelassenen der Schöpfung*, 6th ed. 1976 (ET *Theology of
Joy*, 3rd ed. 1982 [in US as *Theology of Play*]); *Der gekreuzigte Gott*, 5th ed.
1986 (ET *The Crucified God*, 8th ed. 1985); *Kirche in der Kraft des Geistes*,
1975 :(ET *The Church in the Power of the Spirit*, 2nd ed. 1981); *Zukunft der
Schöpfung*, 1977 (ET *The Future of Creation*, 1979); *Trinität und Reich Gottes*,
2nd ed. 1985 (ET *The Trinity and the Kingdom of God*, 2nd ed. 1986); *Gott in
der Schöpfung*, 3rd ed. 1987 (ET *God in Creation*, 1985). *Der Weg Jesu Christi*,
1989 (ET *The Way of Jesus Christ*, 1989).

Hans Küng was born in Sursee, near Lucerne in 1928. From 1948 to 1955 he
studied philosophy and theology at the Papal Gregorian Institute in Rome, and
was ordained in 1954. In 1955 he studied at the Sorbonne and the Institut
Catholique in Paris, and gained his doctorate in theology in 1957. After pastoral
work at the Hofkirche in Luzern, in 1960 he was appointed Professor of
Fundamental Theology in the University of Tübingen. Under Pope John
XXIII he was appointed an official advisor to the Second Vatican Council. In
1963 he became Professor of Dogmatic and Ecumenical Theology and Director
of the Institute for Ecumenical Research in Tübingen. Since 1980 he has held an
independent chair as Professor for Ecumenical Theology as well as continuing as
Director of the Institute for Ecumenical Research. His most recent publications
are *Christianity and the World Religions* (with J van Ess, H. von Stietencron
and H. Bechert, 1984, ET 1985), *Christianity and Chinese Religion* (with
J. Ching, 1988, ET 1989), *Dichtung und Religion* (with W. Jens, 1985);
Theology for the Third Millennium (1987, ET 1988), *Reforming the Church
Today* (1990), *Global Responsibility* (1990, ET 1991) and *Judaism* (1991, ET
1992).